The night and the moment. A dialogue. Translated from the French, of M. Crebillon.

Claude Prosper Jolyot de Crébillon

The night and the moment. A dialogue. Translated from the French, of M. Crebillon.
Crébillon, Claude Prosper Jolyot de
ESTCID: T182205
Reproduction from Cambridge University Library
With a half-title.
London : printed for the translator, and sold by Richarson and Urqhart, 1770.
[4],195,[1]p. ; 12°

Eighteenth Century
Collections Online
Print Editions

Gale ECCO Print Editions

Relive history with *Eighteenth Century Collections Online*, now available in print for the independent historian and collector. This series includes the most significant English-language and foreign-language works printed in Great Britain during the eighteenth century, and is organized in seven different subject areas including literature and language; medicine, science, and technology; and religion and philosophy. The collection also includes thousands of important works from the Americas.

The eighteenth century has been called "The Age of Enlightenment." It was a period of rapid advance in print culture and publishing, in world exploration, and in the rapid growth of science and technology – all of which had a profound impact on the political and cultural landscape. At the end of the century the American Revolution, French Revolution and Industrial Revolution, perhaps three of the most significant events in modern history, set in motion developments that eventually dominated world political, economic, and social life.

In a groundbreaking effort, Gale initiated a revolution of its own: digitization of epic proportions to preserve these invaluable works in the largest online archive of its kind. Contributions from major world libraries constitute over 175,000 original printed works. Scanned images of the actual pages, rather than transcriptions, recreate the works ***as they first appeared.***

Now for the first time, these high-quality digital scans of original works are available via print-on-demand, making them readily accessible to libraries, students, independent scholars, and readers of all ages.

For our initial release we have created seven robust collections to form one the world's most comprehensive catalogs of 18th century works.

Initial Gale ECCO Print Editions collections include:

> ***History and Geography***
> Rich in titles on English life and social history, this collection spans the world as it was known to eighteenth-century historians and explorers. Titles include a wealth of travel accounts and diaries, histories of nations from throughout the world, and maps and charts of a world that was still being discovered. Students of the War of American Independence will find fascinating accounts from the British side of conflict.

Social Science
Delve into what it was like to live during the eighteenth century by reading the first-hand accounts of everyday people, including city dwellers and farmers, businessmen and bankers, artisans and merchants, artists and their patrons, politicians and their constituents. Original texts make the American, French, and Industrial revolutions vividly contemporary.

Medicine, Science and Technology
Medical theory and practice of the 1700s developed rapidly, as is evidenced by the extensive collection, which includes descriptions of diseases, their conditions, and treatments. Books on science and technology, agriculture, military technology, natural philosophy, even cookbooks, are all contained here.

Literature and Language
Western literary study flows out of eighteenth-century works by Alexander Pope, Daniel Defoe, Henry Fielding, Frances Burney, Denis Diderot, Johann Gottfried Herder, Johann Wolfgang von Goethe, and others. Experience the birth of the modern novel, or compare the development of language using dictionaries and grammar discourses.

Religion and Philosophy
The Age of Enlightenment profoundly enriched religious and philosophical understanding and continues to influence present-day thinking. Works collected here include masterpieces by David Hume, Immanuel Kant, and Jean-Jacques Rousseau, as well as religious sermons and moral debates on the issues of the day, such as the slave trade. The Age of Reason saw conflict between Protestantism and Catholicism transformed into one between faith and logic -- a debate that continues in the twenty-first century.

Law and Reference
This collection reveals the history of English common law and Empire law in a vastly changing world of British expansion. Dominating the legal field is the *Commentaries of the Law of England* by Sir William Blackstone, which first appeared in 1765. Reference works such as almanacs and catalogues continue to educate us by revealing the day-to-day workings of society.

Fine Arts
The eighteenth-century fascination with Greek and Roman antiquity followed the systematic excavation of the ruins at Pompeii and Herculaneum in southern Italy; and after 1750 a neoclassical style dominated all artistic fields. The titles here trace developments in mostly English-language works on painting, sculpture, architecture, music, theater, and other disciplines. Instructional works on musical instruments, catalogs of art objects, comic operas, and more are also included.

The BiblioLife Network

This project was made possible in part by the BiblioLife Network (BLN), a project aimed at addressing some of the huge challenges facing book preservationists around the world. The BLN includes libraries, library networks, archives, subject matter experts, online communities and library service providers. We believe every book ever published should be available as a high-quality print reproduction; printed on-demand anywhere in the world. This insures the ongoing accessibility of the content and helps generate sustainable revenue for the libraries and organizations that work to preserve these important materials.

The following book is in the "public domain" and represents an authentic reproduction of the text as printed by the original publisher. While we have attempted to accurately maintain the integrity of the original work, there are sometimes problems with the original work or the micro-film from which the books were digitized. This can result in minor errors in reproduction. Possible imperfections include missing and blurred pages, poor pictures, markings and other reproduction issues beyond our control. Because this work is culturally important, we have made it available as part of our commitment to protecting, preserving, and promoting the world's literature.

GUIDE TO FOLD-OUTS MAPS and OVERSIZED IMAGES

The book you are reading was digitized from microfilm captured over the past thirty to forty years. Years after the creation of the original microfilm, the book was converted to digital files and made available in an online database.

In an online database, page images do not need to conform to the size restrictions found in a printed book. When converting these images back into a printed bound book, the page sizes are standardized in ways that maintain the detail of the original. For large images, such as fold-out maps, the original page image is split into two or more pages

Guidelines used to determine how to split the page image follows:

• Some images are split vertically; large images require vertical and horizontal splits.
• For horizontal splits, the content is split left to right.
• For vertical splits, the content is split from top to bottom.
• For both vertical and horizontal splits, the image is processed from top left to bottom right.

THE

NIGHT and MOMENT.

[Price Two Shillings.]

THE

NIGHT and MOMENT.

A DIALOGUE.

TRANSLATED FROM THE FRENCH,

OF

M. CREBILLON.

Crébillon fils

LONDON:

Printed for the Translator,

and sold by

Richardson and Urquhart, under the
Royal Exchange.

MDCCLXX.

'79... 5520

THE NIGHT AND MOMENT.

THE SCENE IS AT CIDALISA'S COUNTRY HOUSE.

CIDALISA, CLITANDER.

CIDALISA *on seeing* CLITANDER *enter her bed-chamber in his night-gown.*

GOOD God! Clitander, is it you!

CLITANDER.

Your wonder, madam, surprises me not a little; I thought you were accustomed to see me pay my compliments to you, and I can't imagine what it is you find so extraordinary in my present visit.

CIDALISA.

Because I have reason to think I am not the person you would wish to spend the evening with, and, in that notion, I confess your presence surprises me.

CLITANDER.

'Ceremony apart, has it no other effect upon you? is not this visit rather troublesome than wonderful? without being ill-natured, one might think this at least possible.

CIDALISA.

Here is a fancy indeed! will you allow me to ask, what makes you think so?

CLITANDER.

I shall make no mystery of it but will you tell me too, why you are so much surprised at seeing me here this evening, when formerly it seemed a thing so much of course?

CIDALISA.

It appeared to me then that you gave me only your idle hours, but I do not think you are at present so much disengaged as I have seen you

CLITANDER.

I had the same notion of you, and to tell you the truth, I am somewhat uneasy lest you should find my visit a little out of the way.

CIDALISA.

Out of the way! I cannot help admiring the choice and delicacy of your expressions; and, you'll excuse me, the extravagance of your notions: but however, will you have the goodness to tell me, why you imagined you might be so troublesome just now?

CLITANDER.

Yes, if in return you will tell me, why you are so much surprised at this visit?

CIDALISA.

You shall have satisfaction immediately.

[She goes into her closet, returns and shifts herself: her women pull off her shoes and stockings*.]

CLITANDER.

Ah, my God! what a leg!

---

* This is a real and genuine picture of French manners, even in women of the highest quality, and described by a man, no doubt, perfectly acquainted with them. How different these from our manners, even in women whose reputations are equivocal!

CIDALISA.

Oh, have done, my lord! your compliments will not make me forget your assurance.

CLITANDER.

I know not whether this be the first time I have commended it, but I am sure it is not the first time I have admired it.

CIDALISA.

Sit down, I say, or go about your business.

CLITANDER.

You treat me very oddly, madam; but I am all obedience.

[*She goes to bed, ordering one of her women to stay in the room, Clitander seats himself in an easy chair at her bedside.*]

CIDALISA.

What! so Clitander, you have really no appointment with any one?

CLITANDER.

So then I do not hinder you from seeing Erastus.

CIDALISA.

Erastus! But surely you do not think of him, my poor lord.

CLITANDER.

And I swear to you, my fair lady, that I think no more of any of the women, now with you, than you think of him.

CIDALISA.

What! not even of Araminta?

CLITANDER.

Araminta! so, this is pleasant, faith! is it because you had the ill-nature to invite her here, you imagine I must amuse myself with her.

CIDALISA.

An excellent fetch upon my word! that is to say, you would have me believe you know not why she is here.

CLITANDER.

Oh, pardon me as to her hopes I can guess at them, and you may easily perceive it from the chagrin I cannot help feeling at seeing her here. I do not underſtand you; I muſt ſurely be afraid there will be a great dearth of women to take up with ſuch an animal.

CIDALISA.

In truth, Clitander, this is a very needleſs piece of diſcretion, or rather a very ridiculous piece of affectation: you will ſay likewiſe, that it is I who have played you that villainous trick of inviting Celimene, and that it is beſides my fault that Beliſa, Lucinda, and Julia are here at the ſame time.

CLITANDER.

Oh, as for theſe ladies, it cannot be that you think they came here on my account, ſince Cleon, Orontes, and Valere, are alſo your viſitors.

CIDALISA.

But I would not ſwear that you do not ſhare in the honour they do me, for as little as you pretend to it.

CLITANDER.

Nay, this is fooliſh; it is more than eight days ſince I have been here; the gentlemen came

came the day before yesterday; and the ladies to day and it would appear from this arrangement, that you can no more accuse them for having come on my account, than you can flatter yourself with seeing them here upon your own.

CIDALISA.

You surely do not believe me so weak as to flatter myself in that manner.

CLITANDER.

You would besides be in the wrong to complain of Valere, Orontes, and Cleon; they arrived two days before the ladies whom they expected: they are in the grand rules; and I'll engage they would not do so much for the whole world beside.

CIDALISA.

I am sensible of all the politeness of their behaviour, but, Clitander, is it then really true they do not seek you here?

CLITANDER.

You know what they do.

CIDALISA.

But do I know the better for that, what they would do?

CLITANDER.

Ah, madam! allow me to tell you, you ought not to entertain such notions of ladies, whose thoughts are so well regulated as theirs are.

CIDALISA.

Truly, Clitander, you are very ridiculous: but I shall not press you any farther on this head, since I have reason to believe you do not wish it. though I never shall forgive Erastus for coming to spoil an entertainment which would have been so agreeable.

CLITANDER.

Indeed it does not appear very wonderful that you should find him one too many. but I own I do not see, supposing he had not been here, why this supper would have had so many charms for you.

CIDALISA.

What, you do not perceive then how much I should have been diverted at your embarrassment, in the midst of four women, all of whom you have had, and who, without doubt, have still pretensions on you?

CLITANDER.

It would be folly in me to pretend that I have had none of them, but it would surely be greater indiscretion to say I have had them all, besides even supposing they had all honoured me with some marks of their favour, of what consequence is that either to them or to me? How would you have people, whom chance or caprice have brought together for a few days, remember what has been so little interesting to them? What I say is so much the truth, that, supping some time ago with a woman whom I could not recollect by any means, I should have parted with her as a mere stranger, if she herself had not put me in mind that we had formerly been very tender lovers.

CIDALISA.

I am surprised that she should have recollected you. It is said, that we are much apter than the men to forget such sort of adventures.

CLITANDER.

I know you are accused of it but it seems to me, that, in this respect, the failure of memory is equal between the sexes.

CIDALISA.

It is however more singular in a woman than a man.

CLITANDER.

I believe, setting aside prejudices, that this must greatly depend on your having more or less to sacrifice. If, by the greatest chance in the world, a woman should be found that had no more sacrifices to make than ourselves, I do not see for what purpose you would have her call to mind certain things more than us. It is not however so common as perhaps it is thought, that two persons, who have lived somewhat amicably together, however short their connection might have been, however little sentiment may even have entered into it, should remember so little of it, but, at the same time, I do not believe that a total forgetfulness of such things is altogether without example.

CIDALISA.

For my part I could wish to believe it impossible,—you remember Celimene.

CLITANDER.

That is quite another business, our affair lasted a long time, and I loved her too tenderly ever to forget her to that degree.

CIDALISA.

If you speak truth, she is very happy.

CLITANDER.

I doubt it much, since I only remember her to despise her beyond any thing I can express

CIDALISA.

How cruel you are! I have however a commission from her to speak to you.

CLITANDER.

From her, and to me!—after all, nothing from her can surprise me.

CIDALISA.

She pretends you have done her the greatest injustice in the world, and continue obstinate to condemn her without a hearing.

CLITANDER.

You know the story as well as myself, and since you do not think me to blame, you must allow me to be very indifferent about all she can charge me with. I could not even help being surprised, that, being sensible how well you know her, she should have the confidence to desire you to speak to me, had not Erastus, whose unaccountable behaviour to you I have been witness of, likewise, intreated me to intercede with you for him.

CIDALISA.

Seriously, Clitander, has he spoke to you?

CLITANDER.

Yes, madam; and had you seen with what earnestness and vivacity, you would no doubt have been pleased.

CIDALISA.

Oh! highly pleased to be sure; and, according to all appearance, he lays the whole blame of our rupture upon me.

CLITANDER.

Something of that it is natural to think: however, as to his own share in it, I find him pretty moderate on that head; and were it not for your humour, which you conceal, he says, under the mask of delicacy, that you may give yourself up to it with the less scruple, he tells me, you are a good sort of woman enough, and are not altogether void of principles.

CIDALISA.

Insolent fellow! I shall not surely say the same thing of him, but, were you not confounded at the easy familiar air with which he has just settled himself here?

CLITANDER.

It is true, his apparition surprised me a little, yet I could not have believed he would have come here, without being sure you would not take it amiss. That is a sort of respect that ever ought to be observed to a woman of your rank.

CIDALISA.

I think so; but, can you believe it? seven or eight days before my departure, I supped with him at the little countess's; we were talking of the stay we intended to make here, and he had the confidence to tell me, that he would come to wait upon me. As I know he has designs upon that poor little woman, and that she has not as yet entered into his views, I thought that he wanted to make her jealous of me, and did me the honour to believe I had something about me, which might give her the alarm, and determine her in his favour but I received his proposal so coolly, that I own I flattered myself he would not have ventured coming to a place where he knew he must be less welcome than any one else, and that nothing could equal my surprise, when I saw him arrive. Thus I have treated him as you have done, Araminta, who, I think, you would much sooner have than Celimene herself.

CLITANDER.

Faith, in case, as I suspect, you only invited this woman to have some pleasant scenes with her, it must be agreed, that you have succeeded very well, and that our supper has been wonderful pleasant.

CIDALISA.

I do not think, that in my life-time I ever had one so embarrassing and disagreeable. You between two women, whose pretensions are troublesome, for you cannot deny, that there are two at least, who have an eye upon you; myself in the face of Erastus, more out of patience, than I can express at his pretensions, his looks, and his behaviour: no! I really thought I should have died with spleen and anger.

CLITANDER.

We die of these at least every day, and I was not, I assure you, more at ease than yourself.

CIDALISA.

As to your coldness to Celimene, I do not much wonder at it; but, with respect to Araminta, whom you have—

CLITANDER.

Me! have I had Araminta! that is a most abominable calumny.

CIDALISA.

My God! do not be so angry with me; is it my fault, that the publick have given her to you?

CLITANDER.

The publick! the publick, with their good leave, had better keep her to themselves than give her to me, as they have done. That is pleasant enough; the publick!

CIDALISA.

Clitander, you are not a man of honour.

   [*Clitander says something in a very low voice.*]

It is certain, if you continue to speak so low, I shall not be able to hear a word you say. A fine fancy indeed! for what, pray, is all this air of mystery?

CLITANDER [*still very low.*]

Oh, Grisette!

CIDALISA.

Very well, what of her?

CLITANDER.

Oh! nothing at all; only I do not chuse to truſt her with my ſecrets, and cannot, while ſhe ſtays here, explain myſelf freely on ſome certain articles.

CIDALISA.

I do not ſee why you would baniſh her now, for ſome days paſt ſhe did not appear an intruder.

CLITANDER.

That may be, but, ſuppoſing it ſo, I had not the ſame things to ſay to you. You will do as you pleaſe; but I ſhould think, were you to allow us to be alone, it would be ſo much the better.

CIDALISA.

There is a fine notion indeed! Griſette is a very diſcreet girl.

CLITANDER.

I do not attack her discretion, and I doubt not but your secrets may be very safe in her hands. Though you ought not to think it odd, if I do not chuse to trust mine in any body's but yours.

CIDALISA.

She is asleep, and I am sure cannot hear you.

CLITANDER.

She may pretend to be so, and hear me still, in a word, whether she be asleep or not, her presence makes me uneasy. Either permit me to be silent on what you ask me, or consent that we be by ourselves.

CIDALISA.

By ourselves! but for what? indeed it is ridiculous! by no means upon second thoughts, I never will consent to it.

CLITANDER

You'll do as you please, but I confess I am at a loss to understand your backwardness on so simple an affair, which cannot be of

the

the smallest consequence to yourself, and is so necessary to me.

CIDALISA [*a little angrily.*]

Well, it must be as you say; but surely you shew me but very little regard. Grisette! Grisette! see whether she was not asleep. Grisette, you may go to bed.

GRISETTE.

When, madam, should I wait upon you to-morrow?

CIDALISA [*somewhat embarrassed.*]

An odd question that! at the usual hour, I should think.

GRISETTE.

I shall wait till your ladyship rings.

[*She goes out.*]

CIDALISA.

Well, sir, you hear what she says: she has dropt an odd sort of hint though, you see to what you have exposed me.

CLITANDER.

But, madam, condescend to put yourself in my place.

CIDALISA.

Do you put yourself in mine, sir; do you really think she left my bedchamber without the strongest persuasion that she was an eye-sore to us; and that every thing is settled between us, and that this meeting here, which is only an accident, which none of us thought of, is a very serious appointment?

CLITANDER.

She must then be a little malicious hussy, this Grisette of yours.

CIDALISA [*somewhat hastily*]

She is like all others in her way, is not that enough? you yourself, what would you think, were you told to-morrow that one of the gentlemen here had spent the greatest part of the night in my bedchamber? would you have the good-nature to believe that he had done nothing but talk?

CLITANDER.

It is certain, I should believe you had some very particular reason for it but Grisette, who is your confidante, and who knows there is nothing between you and me,

ought

ought not to entertain the same notions of such an affair as I might do. Oh! would to God she might believe me the happiest man in the world, and that I were as much so in reality as she did me the honour to think me.

CIDALISA.
Her absence has made you very gallant.

CLITANDER.
No; but it is strange enough that she has set me more at my ease. If I had been to gain nothing by her going away, of what consequence would it have been to me?

CIDALISA [*in a very serious tone, and a little alarmed.*]
Very well, my lord.—

CLITANDER.
Oh, madam! you know me. Besides what should I gain by failing in my respect to you, if you will grant me nothing I might ask, or if I should offend you by attempting any thing?

CIDALISA.

So, Clitander! you really do not love Araminta?

[*Clitander shrugs his shoulders.*]
However you have *had* her.

CLITANDER.

Oh, madam! that is another matter.

CIDALISA.

Indeed it is said now-a-days it makes a difference.

CLITANDER.

And I believe that it is not now only that it has done so.

CIDALISA.

You surprise me! I thought we had been indebted for that to the modern philosophy.

CLITANDER.

I believe, that in *that*, as well as in many other things, philosophy has corrected our notions. For instance, before we were so well versed in the art of reasoning, we surely

did

did the same things we do now; but we acted, as if carried away by the torrent, without knowledge of the cause, and with that timidity which arises from prejudice. We were not more the objects of esteem than we are now, but we wanted to appear so; and it is evident that such an absurd pretence must have been a dead weight upon pleasure. At last we have had the good fortune to get at truth. At no time have the women introduced into company so little grimace, at no time have they less affected to seem virtuous. People are pleased with one another, and they come together Do they grow tired? they separate with as little ceremony as they met. Do they become fond again? they renew with as much vivacity as if it had been their first acquaintance, they quit one another once more, and yet they never quarrel. It is true, love goes for nothing in all this; but love, what is it but a desire which people have taken a fancy to exaggerate? an emotion of the senses, which the vanity of man has been pleased to rank above the virtues. We are satisfied now-a-days that a taste or likeing only remains; and if we still say we love, it is not so much because we believe it, but because it is a more polite manner of asking one another for what we have mutually occasion for. As people come together without love, they separate without hatred; and one advantage at least arises from this faint likeing which they have conceived for one another, that they are always ready to oblige. Should a woman be apt to sink under the unforeseen inconstancy of her lover, scarce has she time left to think of it, should she be taken with any sudden caprice, it is satisfied on the spot. Should we men be in either of these situations I have mentioned, we find the same resources from the complaisance of women with whom we have lived in any degree of intimacy; and I think, every thing considered, there is a great deal of good sense in sacrificing to so many pleasures, a few old prejudices, which those who make them the rule of their conduct are not much esteemed for, but feel a great deal of trouble and uneasiness from them.

CIDALISA.

Surely, if you believe all you have been just now saying, you have not acted in conformity

to

to your maxims; you who have hardly yet got the better of being jilted by Celimene, and who loved her so tenderly.

CLITANDER.
I adored her, I must confess, and perhaps this is not so much my own peculiar way of thinking, as it seems to be that of many others at present.

CIDALISA.
Ah! whatever chagrin it may have occasioned you, do not change it. It is possible, believe me, that you may meet with a woman worthier of your sentiments, than Celimene has been. And you would have too much to reproach yourself with, should you seek revenge on a deserving mistress for that woman's atrocious behaviour.

CLITANDER.
It is far from being my intention, and if you knew her whom my heart desires, you would not suspect me of a thought, as unjust as it would be barbarous.

CIDALISA.
Then you are no longer in love with Celimene?

CLITANDER.

No, I swear it by all that's good, on the contrary, I know not one for whom I have such a sovereign contempt.

CIDALISA.

Take care, Clitander, you think you hate her, but when one still hates an object one has tenderly loved, the heart is far from being completely cured.

CLITANDER.

I have hated her without doubt, and with a violence, it would be difficult for me to express, but nothing now remains, but that cool and sovereign contempt which none could help feeling for her, who should know as well as I how richly she deserves it that contempt, in short, which you who know her so well entertain for her.

CIDALISA

Can it be Araminta who has so intirely banished her from your heart? I should not easily believe it, and confess I would be sorry for it.

CLITANDER.

Araminta! but, in good faith, can that be supposed? think at least on some woman a man could be a little fond of.

CIDALISA.

But what business has she here, then?

CLITANDER.

I believe I can guess, though it does not follow that I love her.

CIDALISA.

Why then, finding yourself not disposed to treat her better, did you not leave her at Paris? for all joking apart, she has paid me this visit without my having given her the slightest invitation, or even without expecting her, and I tell you frankly, I should be glad of her absence.

CLITANDER.

And I too, I declare, I assure you besides, that if she does not go, I shall go myself.

CIDALISA.

No, Clitander, she will stay, and you must not go.

CLITANDER.

Really, madam, it is odd enough, you should imagine a man can stay in a place where he has the misfortune to find an Araminta, especially when she takes it in her head to be loving.

CIDALISA.

As for that, my lord, I am your friend, and I think you don't question my discretion. Since we have happened to talk of her, open your heart to me, and conceal nothing that has past between you.

[*He muses.*]

What, I pray you, after having confessed you have *had* her, ought you to make so much difficulty in telling me how it came about?

CLITANDER.

You are in the right, and I am sensible I ought not to refuse you what you ask: but these are things, which, whether it be principle, or prejudice, I don't willingly talk of, it is not that I am ignorant that she deserves little ceremony, and that a thousand others can say as much of her as she has put it in my power to say, still—

CIDALISA.

A fine scruple indeed! you have had her, I know it, what then remains but to give me the detail?

CLITANDER.

That is true, and it is precisely for that very reason, that I cannot account for your curiosity. There is so great a sameness in all such adventures, that when you know one, you know a thousand. However, I see you will have it, I shall hide nothing from you.

CIDALISA

But first open that curtain a little more, I do not see you.

CLITANDER.

I went the beginning of last summer to the country, to Julia's, there was a great deal of company there, among others, Araminta, whom nobody wishes to see, and yet who thrusts herself in every where. I was beginning to get the better of my concern for Celimene's inconstancy, and my liberty became every day more troublesome to me. I longed eagerly for a fresh engagement; and, if you will allow me to say so, my heart, which at your first entrance into the world you had so deeply wounded, resumed all its first inclinations for you, but you still loved Eraſtus; and I was too sensible of the vanity of my desires. The certainty of not succeeding, and the fear of becoming troublesome, and displeasing you by pursuing you with that fatiguing perseverance which we think is our duty, when once we have made a declaration, obliged me to keep silence.

CIDALISA.

You did very well; I really loved Eraſtus with the tenderest passion; and you would have had no reason to boaſt of success.

CLITANDER.

I had likewise some reasons to believe that even had you not been engaged, you would not have made me the happier. Be it as it would, I did not even think of letting you know the many acts of infidelity he was daily committing. I was certain

such

such an information would give you an infinite deal of pain; and reflecting on every thing, I thought it best to say nothing, either of my own wishes or his infidelity.

CIDALISA.

Ungrateful man! how I loved him! would you believe it? since he forced me to break with him, it is but a very little time that I have felt for him that profound indifference which cannot be got the better of.

CLITANDER.

In that case he is a fool to stay here any longer, for to conceal nothing from you, he came here to make up matters with you, and he had some hopes of it.

CIDALISA.

That is the drollest thing he has done yet, though I confess I could wish he were sincerely in love with me.

CLITANDER.

Ah! there must be still some love lurking in that wish —

CIDALISA.

I agree that there is reason for such a suspicion, but, I give you my word of honour, that in making it I have not the least thing to reproach myself with.

CLITANDER.

To speak freely, it gives me so much pain to believe you love him, that I most willingly would believe you love him no more. But since we are upon this head, tell me, pray, how a little man of so bad an address, so ill made to please, of such a miserable state of health—

CIDALISA.

Oh Clitander! do not do me the unjustice to think I could pay the smallest attention to that last article!

CLITANDER.

No, to be sure! but it is this, a lover who is a valetudinarian by profession must, as far as I can see, be always less entertaining than another. You grant at least, that if this be not a good reason for breaking with a man, it is certainly a good one for not chusing him at first.

CIDALISA.

Nor was it that which determined me in his favour · good God! what a strange passion is love! when I behold now that same object, which so little a while ago had so much power over me; when I consider that man in cool blood, who has been so dangerous to my heart, I confess, I am at a loss to conceive how he has been able to turn my head in so violent a manner, and I feel, on that account, the strongest indignation against myself.

CLITANDER.

You are then very sure you will never renew with him.

CIDALISA.

What a conceit! at the very time I was dying of grief for having lost him, he attempted in vain to bring me back to him; and my temper is such, that it will not allow me to fear he can do now what he could not then.

CLITANDER [*eagerly.*]

What, then have you thoughts of taking up with any other?

CIDA-

CIDALISA.

By no means, I assure you, but, were I really in love, I flatter myself, I should be able to triumph over my passion, and even leave the object of it in ignorance.

CLITANDER.

Cruel fair! can you really form such designs?

CIDALISA.

Ah! what is that to you?—but resume your story.

CLITANDER.

Do you then think I have nothing more interesting to say to you?

CIDALISA.

I know not; but, you cannot say any thing that will give me so much pleasure.

CLITANDER.

What you say, by the bye, is not very polite, but it affects my heart still more than it mortifies my vanity.

CIDALISA.

Have done then. shall I be in eternal expectation? you are really insupportable.

CLITANDER

Very well. Araminta, as soon as she saw me, set me down for the glorious imployment of amusing her, you know how ready she is at striking up an acquaintance, you know her indecent familiarity, and her coquetish tricks, a thousand times more indecent still. We are all libertines, and I had nothing in my heart to defend me against her. She did not touch me, but she tempted me. I conversed with her in that tone, which alike suited her character, and that sort of impression she had made upon me. So far from being offended, desires, the least flattering for her, and far from being tenderly expressed, appeared a violent passion, which she could not too soon reward. The lively, and scarce decent manner in which I declared my intentions ended in procuring me her esteem. I said very free things to her, and she took them for gallantry. I did not chuse, you may easily believe, to have a regular affair with her, but I thought her

not

not amiss, and I resolved to amuse myself with her, while she stayed at Julia's. One day, returning from a walk, chance led us through a little dark thicket, by the same chance we were insensibly separated from our company. I found the place so very convenient for taking the greatest liberties with her, and herself so well disposed to suffer them, that I know not how she refrained thanking me for it. While she desired me, in the politest manner that could be, to have done, she suffered me to go on with the greatest patience imaginable, in the mean time, she was seized with a fit; and what I shall always reproach myself for, I was so unworthy as to take advantage of the condition I had reduced her to.

CIDALISA.

Ah, good God! how is that! could you—

CLITANDER.

Yes, madam; it was impossible to push the want of respect farther.

CIDALISA.

But, Clitander, by your leave, is the matter really as you represent it?

CLI-

CLITANDER.

They are so simple, that I wonder you can find wherewithal to make a history of them. You know me well enough to be sensible that I am not a common lyar. Besides all this was but a thunder-stroke, and these are become as common of late as it is pretended they were rare formerly.

CIDALISA.

I confess I am not ignorant Araminta has had some affairs on her hands, and that the world does not believe her very cruel, but she is ill-natured enough; her behaviour is light, her tongue no less so. I believed, that scandal had rather been too busy with her, and that she was at bottom more coquettish than loose. You confound me!

CLITANDER.

I am extremely well bred, though I say it, and although she made me no reproaches, yet I thought it my duty, as well as decent, to make her a great many apologies. She received them as a mark of the politest behaviour on my part, and was so charmed with them, that she absolutely would have it I should come, when every body was retired to their repose, and repeat them to her in her bedchamber. We did not begin, as you may see, on the footing of a sentimental affair; and I imagined she had put herself in such a train, that she would not have ventured asking it of me. I must do her justice; at first she thought no more of it than I did myself. We were extreme good company at supper, where she honoured me with all those favours, which a woman who restrains herself only to a certain degree, could confer upon a man in a pretty numerous assembly. I received them as I ought, or rather as I ought not, for I returned them; in the mean time, out of vanity I beseeched her to keep a little within bounds. All t e time after supper she was most execrably tender, at last she retired, and I repaired to her apartment as soon as possible.

CIDALISA.

So you really went!

CLITANDER.

To be sure; what would you have had me do? could I be worse than my word? she
expected

expected me. I found her in bed; and I confess, after all the liberties she had suffered me to take, that I thought going to bed to her could not be very alarming. Indeed, the only thing she asked of me, was to put out the lights, or to draw the curtains. This seemed to be a whim; I do not love them; and I absolutely refused her request. When she saw me obstinate, she had the complaisance to yield to me. The candles were still lighted, and the curtains undrawn. We began to be very familiar together, and I was on the point of being again indebted to her, for the last favours, when a tender inquietude seised her, she called to mind, that I had not yet told her I loved her, and protested, if I did not make her heart easy on that score, that however extraordinary the affection might be she had conceived for me, and whatever proofs she had even already given me of her weakness, that she would undoubtedly overcome it. I was very sensible, that had she loved me, she had no reason to be satisfied with the passion she had inspired me with, but decency, in the condition I was in, obliged me to deceive her; and I answered, I could not imagine, after the actual proofs I had given her of my sentiments, how she could call them in question. Hitherto she had seemed to give way to her tenderness with a sort of restraint; but the certainty of being beloved, banished all her scruples; her fondness, ardour, and vivacity became inconceivable. Ah! if you had seen her, madam—no! that would have been too much!—

CIDALISA [*coldly*.]
I believe it, my lord, but—

CLITANDER.
In a word, though I had at bottom greater reason to complain of her than thank her, I thought that politeness obliged me to make her the gratefullest acknowledgments, and if they did not proceed from the bottom of my heart, I had at least thrown so much gallantry into them, and she was so well satisfied, that she omitted nothing to deserve a repetition of them from me. My God! when I think of it; what a worthy woman she is! however, in spite of all that I owed her, and that sort of giddiness which the first favours of a woman always

always occasion, whether we ought or ought not to receive them with transport, it seemed to me that I should have been still much happier and less indebted to my imagination, if she had had as much reason to boast of the gifts of nature, as she seemed to believe. I have the misfortune to be very curious my doubts tormented me; I intreated her to put an end to them. Nothing could be so easy, nor even so gallant as this request. You cannot however imagine what trouble I had to make her comply. This proposal gave a mortal wound to her modesty.

CIDALISA.

Ah! what a story! this scruple was much apropos.

CLITANDER.

In a word, she would not, and for my part, I would, and whatever resistance she made, I was so determined, that she was at last obliged to yield. Ah! madam,—

CIDALISA.

What then?

CLITANDER.
Ah! what a monster!

CIDALISA.
She! you surprise me! I cannot conceive what that woman can have so horrible about her. her neck and breast are not perfect, but they are not much amiss: she has a well turned arm, a pretty hand enough, and her foot is passable, and I have heard say, all that ought to make us think—

CLITANDER.
Oh, my God! madam, if you knew how little dependance there is upon rules, and how much we are every day one way or other caught by them, you would not be surprised that Araminta should not keep up to what she promises.

CIDALISA.
I am not indeed surprised that before the adventure of the thicket, you should judge of her as I do just now, but I cannot conceive how, after that, you could go to meet her in her chamber, with as much transport as if you had found her altogether charming.

CLITANDER.

If I had the honour to be a little more intimately known to you, you would not aſk me that queſtion. Beſides, after what ſhe had done for me, how could I be off? I had no party to take, but either to give her ſatisfaction, or to make my eſcape: the laſt would undoubtedly have been the wiſeſt; but by ill luck it did not come into my head. Beſides I had not received ſuch accurate information as you might imagine: ſuch rencounters do not allow a nice examination, and if I had no reaſon to think her perfect, I had no opportunity to find her as deteſtable as ſhe is in reality.

CIDALISA.

This is what I cannot underſtand, how a woman, ſuch as you deſcribe Araminta, ſhould be ſo much given to gallantry. Pride ought to ſtand her in the ſtead of principle; for ſuppoſing that on her coming into the world, ſhe thought herſelf poſſeſt of every imaginable charm, it is not poſſible that all the men ſhe has had ſhould have agreed to keep up her vanity; or that if they have had

the

the good manners to preferve fome ceremony, or the infincerity to flatter her, that the fhort time thofe connections fhe has entered into have lafted, and a thoufand other circumftances equally proper to make us open our eyes upon ourfelves, fhould not have undeceived her.

CLITANDER.

We are, upon that fcore, as infincere, or as polite as you think us; and we generally leave a woman without endeavouring to humble her, unlefs our vanity fhould have an intereft in doing it. It is certain, however, that if I had known how ill Araminta's noble confidence in herfelf is founded, I fhould not have *had* her; but I was on this head in the cruelleft fituation in the world. There are few men but what have *had* her, but there is not one of a certain rank who has thought it for his credit to boaft of his happinefs; and fhe is perhaps the woman in France who is beft known, and of whom, at the fame time, we hear the feweft anecdotes: fhe is, in fhort, one of thofe women whom nobody fpeaks of either out of regard to themfelves, or ill-nature againft others.

CIDA-

CIDALISA.
Then you knew nothing of her at all?

CLITANDER.
Excuse me. I knew her, as we all know one another. I had seen her twice at the opera in Julia's box, I had supped with her as often, I believe, at the same lady's, I had met her at court, at the princess's but on all those occasions very little passed between us, and whether my attachment to Celimene was the reason, or she herself had, contrary to custom, some regular affair then on her hands, she behaved to me with an indifference which I could have wished she had had the goodness to continue.

CIDALISA.
I can at present easily believe you. But this intolerable curtain is always falling down; I wish you would manage it so as to give us no farther trouble.

CLITANDER.
If you please, I can do better. You are not a prude, and I am not impertinent, I shall sit down on your bed-side.

[*She makes room for him.*]

CIDA-

CIDALISA.

You must at least acknowledge she has charms that are, in general, sufficiently striking. You understand me, sure?

CLITANDER.

She charms! she has none at all.

CIDALISA.

Oh! for that, Clitander, I cannot believe you; after what you have told me of her transports, her vivacity,—

CLITANDER.

You are deceived; all those transports were no more occasioned by what you think on, than by love, which surely there was none of. It was a compliment she paid me *gratis*, it was pure generosity on her part, or to speak more properly, habit and deceit. She knows we are never pleased with women whom we cannot interest in certain affairs; and she pretended so much ardour only to make me believe that she loved me, and that I might give myself credit for it.

CIDA-

CIDALISA.

Since she has at bottom so little sensibility, what occasion had she to wish for so much ardour in you?

CLITANDER.

She has a very lively and licentious imagination; and though the numberless proofs she has made of a certain sort, ought to prevent her making any more, she cannot be persuaded that she is formed more unhappily than she believes others are, and she always flatters herself, that it is reserved for the last she makes trial of, to render her as sensible as she wishes to be. I doubt not, but this notion is the source of all her dissoluteness, and of the pains she takes to enjoy what she does not feel. Let us add, that these sort of women are very vain, and that, without having the least occasion for a man's being so extraordinary, their pride and vanity wish to see him so, as we from the same motives are sometimes provoked to make efforts which surpass our strength or desires. I shall say more, it is reserved to these days to prove that there are women, who, having

the

the least occasion for the pleasures of love, yet pursue them with the greatest eagerness; and that three fourths of those who have ruined themselves by it, are endowed by nature with all that could preserve them from it.

CIDALISA.

This is what I know as well as you, though I cannot so easily account for it.

CLITANDER.

It is, I confess, a very pleasant age this of ours, and it would be very entertaining to consider it somewhat philosophically.

CIDALISA.

Let us do at this moment, what the age seems always to do, let us not think at all. This wonderful Araminta! pray, did she find you worth all the trouble she took about you?

CLITANDER.

You must believe that I have both very little vanity and a great deal of vivacity, to ask me such a question: how many women are there to whom, in such a case, I would lie most confoundedly!

CIDA-

CIDALISA.

That would be much the same thing to me.

CLITANDER.

So I thought; and to tell you the truth, if she had no reason to look upon the moments she spent upon me as quite lost, she had as little to think them altogether well employed. She, not striking my fancy to a certain degree, I not being so young that vanity should stand me in the stead of a taste she did not inspire me with, you may easily conclude, that the conversation grew now-and-then a little languid between us. Not knowing what to do with this ungainly creature; so sensible of her ridiculous character, as to be no longer amused with it; not being able with decency to quit her so soon, and mortally dreading the spleen, I diverted myself by endeavouring to find out whether she were as singularly tender as she thought herself obliged to appear; spite of all the art with which she acted what she was not, I very soon perceived what she really was. But as women in certain things are extremely capricious; as what appears to one

one unworthy of the flighteft attention is to another a very confiderable object; as there are many who, by a particular turn of mind, prefer illufion to reality; as every one, in fhort, has her own peculiar notions, and even maddifh conceits; I thought, as fincere dealing interefted her fo little, that I fhould try what I could do by trifling and nonfenfe. This refolution was not only the moft reafonable, but, what perhaps will furprife you, feemed to me the moft agreeable. Could you guefs, madam, what I had the honour to fay to her?

CIDALISA.

You do not flatter yourfelf that I fhall anfwer you that queftion? but what was the upfhot of your endeavours?

CLITANDER.

To be fick of the fpleen to death; at laft out of all patience both with her and my foolifh curiofity, I returned to my apartment, fwearing to make no farther trials, at leaft with fo little temptation for them.

CIDALISA.

Had you her for any time?

CLITANDER.

Longer than I ought, five or six days, more or less.

CIDALISA.

What! that woman you thought so horrible! Oh thou libertine!

CLITANDER.

When we returned to Paris, we behaved as if we had only been acquainted at the public Wells. We met oftener than once without having any particular conversation; and without either of us knowing the reason, we were no more than barely civil to each other. At last I met with her at an entertainment, which Philintus gave us at his *petite maison* *. Lucinda, she, Julia, a little provincial girl, a relation of Lucinda's, were the women: the men were Valere, Orontes, Philintus, and myself. Their supper was as insipid as you can well imagine; when it was over we took a walk; we

---

* *Petite maison* is a phrase we have no equivalent for in our language. It signifies a place, either in town or country, set apart for the entertainment of a gentleman's mistress, his friends, and their respective mistresses.

divided

divided the garden amongst us. Araminta, who at supper remembered to have somewhere seen me, and had made me tender enough advances, told me, when we were alone, that she had great news to inform me of, and that a piece of great good fortune had befallen her. I easily guessed what she would be at; and my first notion was, to take her word for it: but we were alone, and I had supped; I remembered that there was nothing on which she deserved any credit, and yet, I could not help trying whether she had told me the truth. Would you believe, madam, that she had told me a lie?

CIDALISA.

I should not have doubted it. So black a perfidy, to all appearance, did not prevail upon you to renew with her.

CLITANDER.

To renew with her! I ought to have beat her; in the mean time, ever since that unhappy night she has thought proper to persecute me; she has resolved that by all the rules I am obliged to love her; she has followed, tormented, and assaulted me everywhere. but let her take care! people are

only

only complaisant to her, because they think her of no consequence; I should ruin her were I to speak out.

CIDALISA.

But, Clitander, do not you pass over some assiduities, some tender letters, some vows of tender love, a thousand things, in short, which the men commonly look upon as nothing; but which we silly women have always the misfortune to reckon upon too much? Is it then really true, that you found no greater charms in possessing her, and that her conquest cost you no more time than you tell me.

CLITANDER.

No, madam, I swear it, sentiment, taste, and pleasure, went for nothing in our affair; and her late behaviour to me is a piece of horrid injustice. On her arrival here she informed me, with a very stately air, that she came to make me explain myself. I answered her with all the respect I profess for her sex, and all the contempt I feel for herself, that there was nothing, about which she and I could have any dispute. When she saw me so well armed against her dignity, she returned to sentiment, and asked it as a favour, that I would spend this night in her apartment, or receive her into mine; and I very cordially assured her, that I would do neither the one nor the other.

CIDALISA.

It was, indeed, the very best thing you could do: and really it was not in her apartment that I concluded you had business tonight.

CLITANDER.

I had none, as you see, but in yours. But to which of the ladies, your visitors, had you thought proper to appoint me?

CIDALISA.

To Julia, I think.

CLITANDER.

To Julia! but is it because I have *had* her?

CIDALISA.

How, if you have *had* her! indeed, the question is admirable!

CLITANDER.

It does not appear to me, I confess, so much out of the way as to you. I think Julia very amiable; but I really wonder you should believe I should have such an intimacy with her, when I never paid my addresses to her.

CIDALISA.

I think, however, I am right in what I say: but what ails you? have you got a fit of the ague, or are you thinking of Araminta?

CLITANDER.

I should not be surprised, if the thoughts of her should produce that effect upon me: for, in truth, I can never call her to mind without being taken with the horrors.

CIDALISA.

You look as if you were dying of cold!

CLITANDER.

That is not very extraordinary; the night is cool, and I have nothing on me but this night-gown, and I begin to find it very thin.

CIDALISA.

I am sorry for it. I want to hear your affair with Julia; and this cross accident shocks me to a degree I can scarcely express. But what could put it into your head to wear a taffatee night-gown? a fine notion indeed! but it cannot be, at least I would fain hope so, that you are quite naked under it.

CLITANDER.

As naked as I was born, and why not? it is now but the beginning of autumn.

CIDALISA [*very cooly.*]

You may do in your own apartment as you please; but you will allow me to tell you, that to come into mine, you have put yourself into a very odd sort of dress.

CLITANDER [*much embarrassed.*]

You have given rise to a reflection which makes me very uneasy; and I cannot express how much I am ashamed of giving you cause to think for a moment, I could have the least intention of failing in respect to you.

CIDALISA [*with a great deal of dignity*]

I imagine, that in this I shew neither humour, nor what they call now-a-days prudery, and which formerly might have past for modesty: but I own to you, I cannot comprehend how you have taken it upon you to appear before me in your present condition.

CLITANDER [*kissing her hand respectfully.*]

Ah, madam! you pierce my very heart. I was but half resolved, since I must tell you, to come to you; I wanted to do it, and I wanted as much to let it alone; I was afraid I should take an improper time; and, if you will allow me to tell you the whole truth, the thoughts of the appointment I supposed you had made, tormented me beyond expression, I was not able to resist my desire, to learn whether you had made one or not. Absorbed in a reverie, I undrest myself mechanically, till at last I took a resolution to venture to your apartment. The confusion of my thoughts! our conversation which began on the spot, and my strong prepossession, did not suffer me to
reflect

reflect on the condition I was in, and in which I have still the misfortune to be, and for which I beg you as many pardons as if I really had designed to offend you.

CIDALISA [*somewhat more moderately.*]

I am very glad to have less reason to complain of you than I thought for, but you will agree with me, I believe, that any other in my place would have thought your behaviour shewed marks of an excessive levity.

CLITANDER.

Nor should I have been much surprised, had any other than yourself supposed me guilty of some intentional want of respect; but you, madam, you who know me, you who are sensible how greatly I esteem you, how could it happen that you should lay me under the necessity of justifying myself from such an imputation?

CIDALISA.

Indeed, I think myself so little liable to contempt, that it will be no difficult matter for you to make me believe, that you do not despise me but let us have done with this and talk of something else.

CLITANDER.

Julia surely is not dying of cold, as I am just now; yet that does not disturb me.

CIDALISA.

It is much the same thing to me, whether you die or not; but whatever may be your case, I desire you, were it only to punish you, to tell me what I was asking of you when you forced me to interrupt you.

CLITANDER.

You are really in earnest then, and want to hear this story.

CIDALISA.

Yes, very much in earnest; I do not deny it.

CLITANDER.

Very well, since you absolutely must have it, I know one means that will put me in a condition of telling it you, if you are agreeable.

CIDALISA.

What is that, pray?

CLITANDER.
But perhaps you will not chuse it.

CIDALISA.
Let us hear it, however.

CLITANDER.
It is——to let me come to bed to you.

CIDALISA.
Nothing but that?

CLITANDER.
Nothing more, I assure you.

CIDALISA.
'Sure, you have lost your wits, Clitander; you take me for an Araminta.

CLITANDER.
I cannot reproach myself with such a gross piece of stupidity, and I swear to you in all good faith and honour what I propose——

CIDALISA.

After what you have told me, it would be a piece of strange inconsistency in me to comply with your request.

CLITANDER.

Ah, Cidalisa! how can you talk of inconsistency, when the question is about saving a man's life?

CIDALISA.

Go, Clitander, you are mad, and fittest for a dark room and straw.

CLITANDER.

But is it possible you doubt of my respect for you?

CIDALISA.

No, I am willing to believe you respect me greatly, and (as the thought of it flatters me so much) I shall surely do nothing to make me forfeit it.

CLITANDER.

Reflect then on what you say. We are alone; all your servants are out of the way, except Grisette, who could be of no great assistance to you, since there is not a person in the world so difficult to be awaked as she is. Your situation is such, that you scarce have any defence against my desires, were I to forget what I owe you so far, as to attempt to offer any thing that might displease you, and yet you see, though I think you the most amiable woman in the world, I have not made you the slightest proposal. I know not why I should be less discreet when in bed with you than I have been out of it. Grant me, I beseech you this favour; I can ask you nothing of so little consequence.

CIDALISA [*angry.*]

Oh, Clitander! you put me out of all patience. I can never consent to it.

CLITANDER.

Very well, then, madam, I must spare you the mortification of giving your consent. [*Here he throws off his night-gown, gets into bed to Cidalisa, and takes her in his arms.*]

CIDALISA [*in a fright*]

Clitander! my lord, if you do not quit my bed, if you do not leave me, if you do not go about your business, I will never see you again while I live.

CLITANDER [*eagerly.*]

But, madam, what would you be at? do not you think your cries may be heard? should any of your servants come in, what would you have them think of the situation we will both be found in?

CIDALISA [*in a rage.*]

What they please. There is nothing I would not expose myself to sooner, than be really the victim of your temerity.

CLITANDER.

Ah, madam! Lucretia herself never thought as you do.

CIDALISA [*in a fury*]

Can I still believe that you are in jest?

CLITANDER.

That would be ridiculous enough, considering the passion I have had the misfortune to put you in; I protest to you, much more innocently than you can imagine.

CIDALISA [*still in the same tone.*]

Go, my lord! it is infamous in you to abuse my friendship as you do. Leave me, I detest you; leave me, I tell you.

CLITANDER.

Well, since it must be so—there you are at your liberty. What have I done to you? I am however in the same bed with you: have you not reason to trust to my discretion, think you?

CIDALISA.

Hold your peace, I detest you! what do you imagine my people will think when they see my bed to-morrow?

CLITANDER.

Nothing at all, madam; I shall make it up again before I leave you.

CIDALISA.

Ay! no doubt that will be a fine work indeed.

CLITANDER.

You shall see. oh! but do not let me be so much the object of your aversion; come a little nearer me, and let the profound tranquillity in which you see me lying beside you, inspire you with some little confidence.

CIDALISA.

You may lay your account, if you make the smallest attempt, with being the object of my eternal hatred.

CLITANDER.

Be it so, may you indeed hate me as much as I could wish you to love me, if you have the least reason to complain of me.

CIDALISA.

I shall not even pardon a proposal, however moderate it may be.

CLITANDER.

That is hard indeed; but it is no matter, I am very willing, let there be no proposals, for then it would be matter of more disgrace to me.

CIDALISA.

You are very welcome to think so.

CLITANDER.

I know not what opinion other people may have of these things, but for my part I never had any pleasure in a refusal. Were we not talking of Araminta?

CIDALISA.

No, we had done with her. But do you really think to ſtay in bed with me?

CLITANDER.

Ah, madam! I thought all that had been ſettled, and that we had entered into conditions with one another.

CIDALISA [*laughing.*]

Though I am certainly very angry at you, yet I cannot help laughing at the oddneſs of this adventure.

CLITANDER.

Indeed, at bottom, I think it wiſer in you to make it an object of pleaſantry than indignation.

CIDALISA.

But, how came you to take it into your head to inſiſt ſo vehemently on coming to bed to one, who does not make you in the leaſt welcome, when there are ſo many others here, who I am ſure would have received you with open arms?

CLITANDER.

I cannot doubt that Araminta, for example, would have very gladly done me that favour; but I believe she is the only one of your visitors from whom I could have expected it.

CIDALISA.

And perhaps the only one from whom you would not have received it. If *Julia, for instance—*.

CLITANDER.

I am really no more tempted by Julia, than by Araminta, or rather, I wish for the one as little as for the other; but it is however true, that if Julia absolutely would have it, I should not be so hard-hearted with respect to her, as to that monster you are speaking of. Is not all that very plain and simple?

CIDALISA.

That is to say, you have found more of that sort of sensibility which is so amusing in Julia, than in the other.

CLITANDER.

But with equal merit in this important article, ought not Julia to have the preference?

CIDALISA.

Undoubtedly. but suppoſing, as you call it, the merit were not equal, I believe it would be difficult to determine, which was the moſt amiable of the two.

CLITANDER.

You are then, it ſeems, convinced that this virtue, when we meet with it in a woman, is really the capital point, and worth all the reſt.

CIDALISA.

Not quite, but I am perſuaded it makes you look over a great many things.

CLITANDER.

It is certain we are the better pleaſed upon that account, generally ſpeaking, for all men are not of the ſame way of thinking.

CIDALISA.

As far as I have been able to observe, you are no less unjust to us on this article than on many others. Is a woman like Araminta? she gives you the spleen. Does she feign what she does not feel? she disgusts you. Is she really sincere? whatever pleasure you may take in that, you are afraid of her. how then must they act in this respect to please you, or not to give you uneasiness?

CLITANDER.

Like yourself, madam. let them have that moderate sensibility which the lover himself is obliged to look for; which is not moved, but by his presence, nor determined but by his caresses, and which any other but himself would in vain endeavour to awaken.

CIDALISA.

May I presume to ask you from whom you have received such admirable intelligence about me.

CLITANDER.

From Erastus, to be sure; for I am not acquainted with Damis.

CIDA-

CIDALISA.

Base fellow! what then, is it true that the men tell one another these things?

CLITANDER.

Yes, when, as it often happens, they have nothing else to say.

CIDALISA.

What a horrible thing it is!

CLITANDER.

I cannot help owning that it is not right; but scarce any of them attack a woman, but out of vanity; and that vanity would not be satisfied with a triumph which no body knew any thing of.

CIDALISA.

How much are we to be pitied, that do not know this!

CLITANDER.

Had it been my case, I should not for my part have made him my confident.

CIDALISA.

Ah! who knows that?

CLITANDER [*eagerly*]

What, Cidalisa, can you doubt it! is there any one whom you honour with your esteem, that you can think capable of such baseness? I must have reparation for this affront. What! won't you answer me?

CIDALISA.

Why, really I do not think you are greatly offended. I would rather, for my part, ask you pardon for thinking worse of you than you deserve, than be obliged to reproach myself for thinking too well of you.

CLITANDER.

That is to say, you do not doubt you would be the victim of any confidence you might repose in me.

CIDALISA.

I believe it is much the same thing to you what I think; and for my part, to tell you the truth, I have not as yet thoroughly settled my notions upon that head.

CLITANDER [*somewhat nettled.*]

Oh, as for that, you need say no more, I have been long sensible, that I am the man in the world the most indifferent to you.

CIDALISA.

I should like to see you make a quarrel of this; would not there be a good deal of vanity in it?

CLITANDER.

I believe, indeed, you would think there were more of that than of sentiment; but, by your leave, it does not follow that you do me justice.

CIDALISA.

Well, well, that is odd enough! so, would you really have me believe you are in love with me?

CLITANDER [*approaching her with a tender and submissive air.*]

But in good faith, do not you believe it yourself?

CIDALISA.

No, upon honour.

CLITANDER [*approaching a little closer.*]

Upon honour, you confound me. I did not flatter myself with your gratitude, but I own, I thought you much better informed.

CIDALISA [*very seriously.*]
A little farther off, I beseech you.

CLITANDER.
What indifference?

CIDALISA [*drily.*]
I know not whether or no it offends you; but I should think you need not be surprised at it. As far as I can see you have formed great projects, and conceived prodigious hopes.

CLITANDER.
I did not think I had behaved in a manner to deserve these reproaches.

CIDALISA.
My God! I know that you deserve none, and I did not think I had made you any; but however, I wish you would go about your business.

CLITANDER.

I should obey you without hesitation, if I did not think my going would be attended with danger for yourself. Araminta will surely come in search of me, and I know not what time she may chuse for her visit. I have reason to fear, that in opening your door I shall find her at mine; and that would be so much the worse, as you know my apartment is directly facing yours.

CIDALISA.

Ah! why did they lodge you there?

CLITANDER.

I know nothing of the matter; surely they would not have done so, unless you had designed that apartment for me.

CIDALISA.

When do you think you shall leave me?

CLITANDER.

How can I know? to-morrow morning perhaps they are not early risers here, I shall go before you are called upon, and no body can suspect I have past the night in your arms.

CIDALISA.
In my arms!———

CLITANDER
Alas! I deceive myself it is you who are in mine, and that is the very thing that makes me the more to be pitied.

CIDALISA
Ah! do not put me in mind of what has paſt between us; I am really aſhamed of it — but I muſt provide againſt every thing, if we ſhould fall aſleep? it is true, Griſette always comes in here firſt———I ſhould, however, be vexed at her finding you here; it would be impoſſible, after having done ſo ſtrange a thing as letting you come to bed to me, for her to imagine I have nothing elſe to reproach myſelf with.

CLITANDER.
Truly, ſhe ought not, and by your fine conduct you won't have ſlept, and will be tired out of your life; and Griſette, to mend the matter, will believe me the happieſt man in the world, and perhaps, ſhe will not keep theſe her conjectures to herſelf.

CIDALISA.

No, upon reflection I cannot submit to that. It is at least doubtful, whether Araminta is gone to your room; besides, the night is far gone, if she intended to go in quest of you, in all appearance she has already done it, and you will not persuade me that she is waiting in the gallery till you have the goodness to open and let her in. No, my lord, once more you must go, I desire you would, and I am resolved you shall.

CLITANDER.

Be it so, madam, since you are willing to run the risk.

CIDALISA.

Oh! the risk you talk of, did it really exist, is nothing in comparison of what you will make me run by staying here.

CLITANDER.

Ah! what are you afraid of from me? such sentiments as you inspire are not apt to make a man so very bold.

CIDALISA [*with an air of raillery.*]

Your sentiments!———

CLITANDER.

That is to say, you do not believe I love you.

CIDALISA.

No, surely I do not believe it but to-morrow I may be better disposed than to-night, to tell you my thoughts on the state of your heart. In the mean time, you will do me, I repeat it, the greatest pleasure in the world to quit my bed, and I could wish you would not oblige me to tell you so any more.

CLITANDER [*eagerly.*]

Forgive me, if I oblige you to tell me so again and again, the happiness of my present situation with you is so very inchanting, in spite of the restraint you have laid me under—Ah, madam, what a thought! is it possible that I am lying with the finest woman in the world, with her whose favours are of all others the most ravishing! that I should hold her in my arms! that I should clasp her in them! that there should be only between her and me the slightest impediments, and that she will not suffer me to break through them!

CIDALISA.

That is, indeed, a piece of great cruelty in me!

CLITANDER.

What then, will you always repay my assiduities with this dreadful indifference?

CIDALISA.

I never had reason to believe that they were serious. I know, indeed, that I may have sometimes given you desire; but, Clitander, desire is not love, although you may express both in much the same manner; I know the world too well to be deceived. No, I tell you you do not love me; and a thousand women have made the same impression on you.

CLITANDER.

How happy you are to believe so! cruel woman!

CIDALISA.

Clitander, we have been friends too long that I should practise with you all those little tricks which we generally think we owe to the decency required of our sex, and which at bottom we never make use of, but to satisfy our coquetry, for your part, let me have no more of that idle jargon and deceit with which you make every day so many dupes. It would be infamous in you to speak of love to me without feeling it, and I think I may say, setting our friendship aside, I am intitled to another sort of behaviour from you. Either you do not love me now, or, what I have great reasons to disbelieve, you have loved me for a long time.

CLITANDER.

Yes, madam, I have loved you ever since I had first the happiness of seeing you.

CIDALISA.

In that case, you must allow you have taken delight in giving yourself up to dissipation; for without mentioning such women as Araminta, with whom you have amused yourself at different times, you have *had*, since we were acquainted, Aspasia and Celimene. You have loved them both very tenderly. nothing but the death of the first could have broken those ties which united you

you to her, and if the other had not been guilty of the blackeſt perfidy, you would have *had* her ſtill. It is, allow me to ſay, very odd, that having loved me ſo long, as you would make me believe, you could attach yourſelf ſo ſtrongly to others, and that you never opened your heart to me.

CLITANDER.

Ah! how could I have done it? when we were firſt acquainted, you were deſperately fond of Damis; he quitted you. I was in Italy, when I returned, Eraſtus had attached himſelf to you: if you had him not then, he had already become agreeable. What time then could I take to ſpeak of my paſſion?

CIDALISA.

You did well to ſay nothing about it, ſince you believed me engaged, but perhaps you would have done better, not to have believed that ſo eaſily. It is, beſides, very natural for me to think, that if you had loved me, you would have endeavoured to make a diverſion; it is at leaſt what another would have done: but every one has his own maxims.

CLITANDER.

I have the same as all the world on that score, and you would have found me as importunate at least as Erastus, if you had not given so cold an answer to the letter I wrote you from Turin, on the inconstancy of Dam's, and if you had seemed to pay the smallest attention to the offer I then made you of my heart.

CIDALISA.

Indeed! it is very strange, that at the very time I was dying with grief for the infamous behaviour of a man to whom I had been attached since my first entrance into the world, I should not have given a favourable answer to proposals tender enough, it is true, but which I thought I must impute rather to politeness than love.

CLITANDER.

You would have imputed them to their real cause, had they had the good fortune to please you. No, madam, my love would have been troublesome, and without doubt, may be troublesome to you still.

CIDALISA.

That is very possible; my present tranquillity pleases me. The two trials I have made, ought not to make me disposed for a new engagement; and besides, I am not of that way of thinking, to pass perpetually from the arms of one man into those of another. Very young as yet, I have had the misfortune to have two affairs; I despise myself for it. The world was angry at the inconstancy of Damis, which I certainly did not deserve: but it blamed me for taking up with Erastus, and with a heart tender and sincere, having no other fault, but weakness, I was, perhaps, thought dissolute, or at least born with strong dispositions to become so. I ought, and am resolved to suffer myself to be forgotten.

CLITANDER.

Ah, madam! when you took up with Erastus, it was not for having a new passion that the world blamed you, for do you think that the choice of the object goes for nothing? it is perhaps a piece of tyranny; but in a word, people require that what appears amiable to us us should also please them, and do not forgive us for putting a certain value upon what they have not thought proper to esteem; and you cannot be ignorant, that Erastus has not acquired the esteem of the publick. I could even venture to say, had you made choice of me, they would have spoke of it in a different manner. Erastus may have an advantage over me in the agreeable qualities; but I dare affirm, that my principles and way of thinking are viewed in another light than his, and I need no other proof of this, than what has happened to Celimene, who is perhaps become more infamous for having quitted me, than Araminta for giving herself up to all the world. Your present disposition will not last for ever. You are naturally tender; and if the misfortunes you have met with have made you afraid of love, they have not destroyed in you the necessity of loving. I think I owe you so much consideration as not to be troublesome with my passion, but if ever you choose a fresh engagement, do not forget, I earnestly beseech you, that I have asked the preference.

CIDA-

CIDALISA.

We shall see by that time. All that I can at present, or indeed think I ought to say, is that you are the man in the world I esteem the most, and I will not even doubt I should have been as happy with you as I have been the contrary with those two unworthy mortals I yielded myself up to.

CLITANDER [*tenderly kissing her hand.*]

Ah, madam! how happy you make me! may I then, at last, talk to you of my passion?

CIDALISA.

Not a jot the more for that, I should think; you have this moment engaged never to speak of it, and this is a promise, which you will take notice, I shall by no means dispense with.

CLITANDER.

Ah! could you think that it was serious, and that I can keep silence on a passion so long confined within my own breast, since I may flatter myself, that, in breaking it, I will not displease you.

CIDALISA.

I do not believe I told you so much, but for God's sake, let us have done with this subject you are not dying of cold at present, and you oblige me to put you in mind that you owe me Julia's history.

CLITANDER.

Indeed! it alarms me greatly, madam, that you still remember there is such a person in the world. besides, I have nothing to say of Julia, not I.

CIDALISA.

Ah! what reserve! I am glad of it though, you may look for the like from me.

CLITANDER.

Once more, madam, I have nothing to say of Julia besides, if you knew with what a bad grace I relate matters of fact in bed, you would not surely think of transforming me there into an historian.

CIDALISA.

All these excuses are to no purpose; we either talk of Julia, or of nothing at all. How long is it since you have *had* her?

CLITANDER.

You are, allow me to say so, strangely obstinate! but, supposing that I have *had* Julia, and that there were something in our affair very pleasant, and which distinguished it from all others of the same sort, yet it would actually be a history the worst placed of any in the world.

CIDALISA.

For you, perhaps.

CLITANDER.

And so much so, that if this night's adventure were committed to writing, and, while we are in our present situation, such a history should come in, there is not one, but would pass it over without hesitation, whatever pleasure he might promise himself from it.

CIDALISA.

That will be according to the taste and ideas of the reader.

CLITANDER

There are none, I believe, who, for the sake of a long tale, would wish to cut the thread of such an interesting situation.

CIDALISA.

I do not see, for my part, what there is so very interesting in our present affair. I confess, it may be extraordinary, and that it is not very common, for a man with an air of authority to go to bed to a woman, who is by no means disposed or expected to suffer such liberties to be taken with her; people would not think it very probable, and they would do well, it might appear still less so, that she should allow it. but for an interesting situation, I do not see——

CLITANDER.

Very well, madam; though all you say were true, I can no longer endure the ridicule of telling you stories, when I ought to be speaking to you only of my passion, and endeavouring to prevail on you to make it a suitable return.

CIDALISA.

Have you then, very seriously, formed such a project?

CLITANDER.

Yes, madam; and it is not of this night only.

CIDALISA.

I think I have some reasons to be of another opinion, and were not the night so far gone, I might tell you what they are; but I am very sleepy, and I could wish you would leave me to my repose.

CIDALISA.

Consider, I pray, how inconsistent you are.

CIDALISA.

That is a point I do not choose to enter upon; inconsistent, even unjust, worse still, if you will, I have no objection, provided you will but quit my bed.

CLITANDER.

Did you but know now what a desire I have to do no such thing!

CIDALISA.

That, indeed, may be; but I do not think that on this occasion I have any business to consult either your desires, or aversions.

CLITANDER.

Well, but now let us talk seriously; what will you give me not to tell any body I have lain with you?

CIDALISA.

That is a piece of very silly buffoonery, my lord, do not let us trifle any more on this subject. When I reflect on my foolish complaisance——

CLITANDER.

And I on my weakness!—but I have this to comfort me, as it is actually incredible, no body will believe it; and in so great a folly as I have committed, it is, however, some consolation that my reputation is safe.

CIDALISA.

I understand you; that is to say, you will not be silent on this adventure, and will not fail to boast you have pushed it as far as possible, and have used me without the smallest ceremony.

CLITANDER.

I do not believe though, what I have juſt now ſaid can bear that meaning. But as that has come on the carpet, will you be ſo good as grant me ſome favours?

CIDALISA.

Some favours! ah! I either grant you all or none.

CLITANDER.

All! well then be it ſo.
> [*Here he loſes all reſpect, very indecently; ſhe defends herſelf furiouſly, and baffles him.*]

CIDALISA [*with a cold and angry air.*]

I ſee, my lord, though you have lived with me a long time, you are not the better acquainted with me. For all that I ſhall not defend myſelf by ſcreaming, which would only make my folly publick; and as I am neither a ſtarch prude, nor looſe coquette, as conſtitution, and the pride of virtue, have no weight with me, I ſhall make no noiſe,

but

but you shall not *have* me, and if you really think of me, you will have the mortification to see me break with you for ever. You are therefore to consider on the part you are to take.

CLITANDER.

Ah! madam, how far am I still from the happiness you seemed to promise me? and if you thought of me, as you told me you did, how little would you be offended at all that my love could attempt. Ah! have not I given you every possible mark of my respect? I adore you! were my passion for you less ardent, you are handsome, I am young, my situation with you is, perhaps, the most painful situation a man can be in. I die with love and desire, and you doubt it not; yet have not I been as discreet as you conditioned with me to be? have my hands so much as wandered? have I made any bad use of yours? master as I am, in many respects, of the finest woman in the world, have not you found me as moderate as I would be with that execrable Araminta, for whom I have such an aversion? I want no recompence, and I do not wish you to believe you owe me any favours, for this reason only, that

that I have not attempted to ravish any from you, but let my self-denial, too severe to arise from any other motive than the most ardent love, convince you at least of its truth and sincerity.

CIDALISA.

I wonder at you men, and reflect with terror on the power that a critical moment has over them! When you came here first, you had no intention to shew yourself so very loving, and though possibly you may always have had a sort of taste for me, and I might even believe, that it has increased since you saw me at liberty, yet I have more reasons than one, to think I do not inspire you with a real passion. But you are disengaged, and alone with me to-night, and by an imprudence I shall never forgive in myself, which is scarce credible, and which even I cannot help still doubting of, I have suffered you to come to bed to me. Though I should be much less agreable in your eyes, I should still give you desires, and particularly of triumphing over me at the present moment, that you might have so singular an adventure to boast of. Own at least, that if I give you credit for

for some motives, I owe a great deal to the *moment*, for that violent passion you would have me believe you possest with.

CLITANDER.

It is not of to-day, madam, that I am to learn people are as ingenious in finding reasons against what is disagreeable to them, as expert at invalidating those which oppose their favourite passions. You are not ignorant, though you seem to entertain such a disadvantageous opinion of me, that I have never been so foolish as to covet the character of universal gallantry, nor to attempt women whom I had no value for, merely for the vain-glory of conquest: you have formerly done me that piece of justice; but the times are changed; and it would be in vain for me to expect so much from you now, unless I were to be as indifferent about you as you desire.

[*Here he kisses her hand with tenderness and respect, and continues doing so, till she makes him a reply. On her side, she listens with great attention, and an air of great embarrassment.*]

Ah! madam, why do you rack your invention to accuse me? why do you so cruelly repay my passion with contempt? you do

not

not love me: is it possible for you to think you have not made me sufficiently unhappy? you reproach me for my silence: what! is it because I never ventured to tell you I loved you, that you can doubt of it? Alas! at what time was it, I could flatter myself such a declaration would not have displeased you? Was I ignorant of your engagements? and ought I to have imagined you would forgive me, for believing you inconstant or perfidious? I behold you free at last, and happy enough to be so myself, I might, it is true, have talked to you of my passion, but too deeply affected not to be always in fear, my eyes alone have ventured to make you acquainted with it. I thought, before I discovered it, it was my duty to dispose your heart to receive it. You have seen me following you like your shadow, preferring you to every thing else, frequenting those places only where I had hopes to meet you, and sensible to no other pleasure, but that of passing my time with you. Very well, madam, continue still to hate me: you shall see me still constant and submissive, preferring even the hardships you make me suffer to those favours I might expect from others.

others. Does my love displease you? I consent to say no more about it, provided you will permit me to give you continual proofs of it by my actions.

CIDALISA [*with emotion.*]
Ah! traitor, must I at last be so unhappy as to wish you are now sincere?

[*Here Clitander clasps her in his arms, while she makes but a faint resistance.*]

CLITANDER.
Cidalisa, my charming Cidalisa, if you pleased, how happy could you make me!

CIDALISA.
Ah! do you believe you would be long so? To give you my heart, and all that I know I should give you with it, would it not be falling back into that dreadful situation out of which I have but just escaped; still deeply affected with the remembrance of my past unhappiness? I cannot help looking on love with horror, and would fain hate you for endeavouring to please me, and for being perhaps too successful in these endeavours.

CLITANDER [*drawing nearer to her.*]

Vouchsafe, I beseech you, to banish these melancholy notions! let what I have hitherto been give you confidence for the future; turn your eyes upon me, and keep them there, if possible, without uneasiness. [*Here she sighs.*] Will these cruel fears never be dispelled, and will you still persist to despond because you find yourself in my arms?

[*She still sighs, looks at him tenderly, and draws nearer him; but finds him far from being so respectful as he had promised to be.*]

CIDALISA [*defending herself.*]

Ah!—Clitander!—what are you doing?—If you love me!—Clitander!—let me alone, I command you.

[*He obeys at last. She weeps, and removes farther from him with great indignation.*]

CLITANDER [*peevishly.*]

I perceive, madam, too late, that carried away by my passion, and vainly flattering myself that you did not disapprove it, I have

have had the misfortune to incur your displeasure. The grief that my boldness occasions you, has, however, taught me that I am the last man in the world to whom you would grant those favours I have just now ravished; and I do not conceive how I could have been so blind on this matter so long.

[*She makes him no answer, and he is likewise silent, but sighs, at last, finding he continues so.*]

CIDALISA [*very drily, and without looking at him.*]

I believe, my lord, it is time you should leave me to my repose.

CLITANDER.

Yes, madam, I think so too. I shall do even more than you seem to require; I shall leave you for ever.

CIDALISA.

Go, my lord! and may you forget my imprudence, and neither make a crime of it to yourself, nor to any one else.

CLITANDER.

Ah! madam, I cannot be worthy of your affections, but always shall of your esteem; and your treatment of me, cruel as it is, shall never root out from my heart the profound respect I bear you.

CIDALISA [*ironically.*]

I love to hear you talk so, after treating me in this manner.

CLITANDER.

I shall not endeavour to apologize for a thing that has displeased you; though it might not perhaps be very difficult to justify it; but you will have me in the fault, and I should believe myself so indeed, if I attempted to make you sensible of your own injustice. I leave that to time, and I pray heaven it may not give me my revenge. Farewell, madam, I am going——

[*He seems as if he were seeking for something.*]

CIDALISA [*still without looking at him.*]

What are you seeking for, my lord?

CLITANDER.

My night-gown, madam, for on the footing we now are together, I do not think it would be decent for me to appear before you *en deshabille*.

CIDALISA [*still coldly.*]

You are somewhat of the lateſt in obſerving this decorum with me ſtay, my lord, you have thrown it by me, I ſhall give it you preſently.

CLITANDER [*approaches her with transport.*]

Cruel fair! is it then true, you can loſe me with ſo little regret; and that the man in the world, who loves you the moſt, ſhould labour under your fixt averſion?

CIDALISA.

Alas! my lord, you know but too well I do not hate you.

CLITANDER.

So, then, is it poſſible that I am deceived! that thoſe charming eyes in which I read lately ſo much indignation, ſhould ſpeak to me in a softer language. [*She smiles on him with tenderness.*] Yes, Cidalisa, I once more perceive in them some marks of that goodness with which they so lately flattered me, but how far are they still from those sentiments which mine express, and for which I cannot procure an entrance into your heart!

CIDALISA [*after a short silence.*]

You will absolutely have it then, that I should love you: very well, cruel man! enjoy your victory: I adore you!

CLITANDER.

Ah, madam!—joy chokes me, I cannot speak.

[*He sighs, and falls on Cidalisa's neck, and remains th re for some time motionless.*]

CIDALISA

Behold at last those cruel affections which have hitherto caused the unhappiness of my whole life, have returned to take possession of my heart. Ah! why have you
raised

raised them up again in me? alas! I was ignorant, or rather wanted to be so, of the nature and strength of that passion which drew me towards you, and perhaps I might have triumphed over it, if you had not made it your business to seduce me.

CLITANDER [*eagerly.*]

It is too much; I can no longer resist so many charms! oh! let me expire in your arms.

CIDALISA.

One moment, I beseech you Clitander: you know me, since I have at last consented to give you my heart, you ought not to doubt, that you will one day be master of my person, but suffer me to accustom myself to my weakness, and let me, at least, have the consolation not to fall like that unhappy wretch, whose enormities you have just been giving an account of.

CLITANDER.

What! can you then be afraid I should confound you with her?

CIDALISA.

Were I so happy as to have had you for my first engagement, and were you better acquainted with my way of thinking, you should neither meet with those fears nor scruples, but I do not bring you a virgin heart: and whatever value you may set upon it now, I tremble lest you may not always esteem it so much, and that the little trouble it has cost you, may render it one day very contemptible.

CLITANDER.

Can you suspect me of thinking ill of you, or doubt my esteem? yes, you do; for you have told me, that I take you for an Araminta, a hint of that sort must surely be very agreeable to me!

CIDALISA.

It is perhaps but too true, and the manner of my yielding——

CLITANDER.

Ah! why will not you yield? you love me; though you have not told me so, till just now, yet before now I began to see it.

Your confidence in me; the sacrifices you have made me, without my having asked them, or perhaps yourself being sensible of them; that sort of spite which, gentle as you are, you have conceived against those women, whom I may have been too often with, or seemed to think too well of; your apprehensions that I should not come here; the earnestness with which you have always asked me to come; your good humour at seeing me here; the ill humour that seised you on the arrival of these women, the many anxious and troubled looks you have given me on their account; must not all this have made me acquainted with your passion? Can you believe, that with such dispositions, habituated to me by our long friendship, less on your guard of course against the liberties I took, sure of being loved, equally prest with your own love and mine, you could resist my ardour; and ought you to compare what passes between us to what has past between Araminta and me?

[Here perhaps it may not be amiss to inform the reader, that while Clitander is speaking he caresses Cidalisa in the tenderest

derest manner; which, she neither altogether returns, nor opposes, beyond a certain degree.]

CIDALISA.

[*In answer to what he has said, rather than to what he has done.*]

To speak freely, there is nothing I think less of; and the only thing I can really have any pleasure in believing, is, that I could not have done otherwise than I have done. I must however be mistaken, for you cannot imagine what difficulty I have to persuade myself of it.

CLITANDER.

You are only the dearer to me, on that account; but, however much I approve your delicacy, I should be sorry you should make use of it to torment yourself.

CIDALISA.

Alas! can I be as easy as you would have me, when I think that one day perhaps you may find more reasons for blaming my conduct, than you now have for excusing it.

[*He answers her only by making attempts, she is silent, but makes a vigorous resistance.*]

CLITANDER.

Indeed, Cidalisa, you are to the last degree unreasonable. You do not love me then.—

[She clasps him tenderly in her arms.]

But how would you have me believe you, when I see you pay more attention to your fears than to your tenderness, and give the lye by your behaviour to all you have been swearing with your lips: grant at least something to my desires.

CIDALISA.

You cannot surely restrain them; and perhaps I shall not have strength to put a stop to them.

[Here he asks for something, which is however next to nothing.]

CIDALISA.

Good God!—will you keep your word then, and pay a proper regard to my fears?

CLITANDER.

Yes, since I find I cannot get the better of them.

[Here

[*Here she consents to what he had asked, and, as she had foreseen, and perhaps hoped, he is worse than his word. The reader will easily believe she is vexed at his being so at the time.*]

CIDALISA [*with majesty enough.*]
Ah, my lord! you know our agreement.

CLITANDER.
Except that of always loving one another, I know of none between us; but leave off, I beseech you, that air and manner which are not proper for us. The ceremony you still treat me with makes me almost doubt your having told me you love me; and I cannot express how much I am vexed at it.

CIDALISA [*with transport.*]
Ah! you ought not to doubt my tenderness one moment, and I shall be too happy to see you always as well satisfied of it, as you will always have reason to be so.

CLITANDER.
You kiss me, however, without pleasure; and while my heart flies to my lips, and is pierced with the softest ecstasy, you seem

either

AND MOMENT.

either to deny yourself the same happiness, or to be incapable of feeling it.

CIDALISA.

How can you take delight in drawing such an unfaithful picture of my emotion!—confess now you are in the wrong.

[Cidalisa's transports authorising in some sort Clitander's rashness, he asks her for certain favours, which though not the highest that may be exacted from a woman, are still, however, pretty singular; she refuses them: he asks them again, but meets with a fresh refusal: he is nettled at this, and uses his authority with an insolence that may be thought without example, or at least not very common, and ought to teach the ladies not to suffer a man to go to bed to them so inconsiderately.

CIDALISA *[desperately angry.]*

No, I will not—you offend me mortally! so then!—there you are.—Very well! there! how could I trust you?

[These violent reproaches are so far from restraining Clitander, and Cidalisa's resistance, which we must believe to be very

very sincere, is so far from having any influence upon him, that he still continues to use violence; it succeeds at last; for what could she do, and where is her remedy? it is true, she calls him a very impertinent fellow; but when once a man has taken upon himself to be so, there would be very little merit, and it may be still worse policy, in ceasing to offend. He continues therefore to make a bad use of his superior strength, however unbecoming that may be; at last he smiles upon her with an air of as much satisfaction as if he had performed the finest feat in the world, and he wants even to kiss her hand It may easily be believed, after what she has to reproach him with, that this mark of acknowledgment, however full of respect, is very coldly received.]

CIDALISA [*inraged, and in a very terrible tone.*]

Leave me, I desire you, my lord; I am out of all patience with you, your behaviour is detestable.

CLITANDER.

Do but see to what a height you carry your injustice. Could you imagine, setting
even

even love aside, that, being bleſt with the careſſes of ſuch a woman as you, the moderation you preſcribed me, was in my power. Beſides, of what do you complain? have not I greater reaſons to be offended at you for refuſing me favours ſo common? You are indeed very ſingular in your way.

CIDALISA.

No doubt, I ſee very well, I ſhall be always in the wrong. This is not, however, what you promiſed me.

CLITANDER.

Believe not, I beſeech you, that in that reſpect I was ſo inſincere, as to promiſe you any thing. Conſider, that in our preſent ſituation, it is impoſſible I can be impertinent to you; and when it is yourſelf, who offend love, do not think that I hurt your dignity.

CIDALISA [*a great deal more gentl.*]

But, my God! can you imagine I am ſo blind as not to foreſee I ſhall one day do more for you than you have at preſent exacted of me? You are in the right; if my reſiſtance had no foundation, it would be

K

to the laſt degree ridiculous, but whatever may be its motives, you have promiſed, ſay what you will, to reſpect them; and I think at leaſt, I have a right to complain of your being worſe than your word.

CLITANDER.

You are then very angry. Ah! return to my arms; I am dying with eagerneſs to pardon you all your faults. Come, do not withdraw from my clemency.

CIDALISA [*laughing*]

Indeed, you are ſtrangely ridiculous! Ah, Clitander! I perceive you well.

[*In all appearance ſhe has here ſome reaſon for ſpeaking as ſhe does.*]

CLITANDER.

You won't go to be angry again, will you?

CIDALISA.

At bottom, I ſhould have reaſon; but I ſee, at the rate you go on, I ſhould have nothing elſe to do, and were it only to catch you tripping, I have ſome inclination to be a little leſs cruel.

CLITANDER.

To catch me tripping! where have you learnt that, if you please?

CIDALISA.

Is it then really true, I am so much in the wrong?

[The reader will here be so good as to take this question to himself. If by chance, which indeed can scarce be believed, some woman should read this part, she ought to learn from thence never to affront any man without very good reason; that is to say, she ought to be aware of speaking on certain occasions from bare probabilities, in which it is possible she may be mistaken, and when she shews any offensive doubts, she cannot be too physically certain for fear of consequences.]

[Clitander proves to Cidalisa, who had at first asked him pardon, and is afterwards extremely vexed at it, that she had done better, if she had testified no such doubts of his abilities It is to no purpose she tells him

him such a harmless pleasantry ought not to be attended with consequences so very serious. Whether he is really piqued at it, or pretends to be so, it is certain he takes his full revenge. After all, however, it is necessary that this should have an end, one way or another, and that she should complain of him, as much as perhaps. she was secretly pleased. Clitander owes the tenderest acknowledgments to Cidalisa, and actually makes them. As it cannot be supposed, that there are any of our readers, who are not, or have not been in the situation of giving or receiving, of saying, or hearing all those passionate and flattering suggestions of grateful love, or what the necessity of being polite sometimes dictates, we shall omit the conversation of the two lovers, in this place, and we shall venture to say, that the reader will have very little reason to complain of it, because he is only deprived of some few broken exclamations, which he will have more pleasure in composing for himself, from his own

ideas

ideas or memory, than he would find in reading them here.

It is very true, that there may be some, who not knowing either how to give or receive thanks on such occasions, may be displeased at not meeting with information here, but we do not choose to render nature artificial in the one, or to be so cruel as to deprive the other of the pleasure of surprize.

CLITANDER [*laying himself beside Cidalisa, who dares not look at him, at least not without confusion.*]

What then, my charming Cidalisa! will you always reproach, or rather punish me, for having made myself happy? I am to blame no doubt; but if you do yourself justice, you will find, not only many reasons for pardoning my fault, but even some for wondering I have not committed it sooner.

[*She says nothing, sighs, and will not look at him. He goes on—*]

Lift then your charming eyes upon me; let them tell me, since your lips will not, that you do not hate me. I cannot a moment survive the fear of having displeased you. Would you really have me die of grief?

[*He kisses her hand very tenderly.*]

CIDALISA [*still angry.*]

Ah, traitor!

CLITANDER.

Be it so; heap upon me every reproach you can imagine, without doubt I deserve them all, but yet look upon me once more; tell me, I beseech you, what makes you so uneasy?

CIDALISA.

Alas! how can I help tormenting myself with the apprehensions of losing you?

CLITANDER.

Ah! do not give way to such ill-grounded fears. I adore you! nothing was ever so dear to me, and nothing shall ever be so much so.

CIDALISA [*looking at him with extreme tenderness.*]

Is it really true, that you love me still!

[*Clitander endeavours to banish those fears of Cidalisa no otherwise than by stifling her with the most ardent caresses. But, as every one may not have his method of removing doubts, such of our readers, who do not think that so convenient, may take any other course, such as making Cidalisa the finest and most gallant speeches imaginable; in short, doing any thing they think could satisfy a lady in her situation.*]

CLITANDER.

Well then, ungrateful woman, are you satisfied?

CIDALISA.

Ah, Clitander! what a pity it is, I can so well distinguish between desire and love.

CLITANDER.

That is to say, you still doubt of mine.

CIDALISA [*sighing.*]

This doubt is not so unreasonable as you would seem to believe, but you answer it in such a manner, as to oblige me to keep it to myself, you do not, however, destroy it.

CLITANDER.

Would you give more credit to my oaths?

CIDALISA.

That manner of expressing your passion might not be so amusing or so flattering to your vanity, but I confess, however deceitful it might be, it would set my heart more at ease than those transports you substitute in its room.

CLITANDER [*tenderly.*]

Ah! how can you, for a moment, imagine I have not the greatest pleasure in disclosing those sentiments which ingross my whole heart, and which I now think I feel for the first time in my life.

CIDALISA.

No, no, I have cost you too little for me ever to be so happy as you say. In truth, you are somewhat unreasonable.

[*Cidalisa kissing his hand with transport.*]

You know not how much I love you! how much I abhor myself, for having been any one's but your's! how much I even

hate

hate you for having loved me so late! and when indeed I reflect that you might have prevented me the misfortune of having *had* Erastus, can I do otherwise than detest you for suffering me to take up with him?

CLITANDER.

Erastus! was he not already your favourite when I returned?

CIDALISA.

No, he was then only endeavouring to be so; and if you had at your return confirmed all you had wrote, he would have still sought it in vain.

CLITANDER.

Ah! if I had thought it! but how could I imagine you were so favourably disposed as to my passion, when I saw you colder and more reserved to me than to any one else, and that you scarce shewed me any marks even of common friendship.

CIDALISA.

A desire to avoid all engagements of any sort, and an apprehension that you would be more prejudicial to that resolution than any

other,

other, were the first causes of that coldness I shewed you on your return, and the grief to see you renew with Celimene, when, spite of my heart, I still flattered myself you loved only me, inspired me with such a violent hatred against you, that I know not yet how I got the better of it.

CLITANDER.

I confess, that I have not been altogether in the dark as to your real sentiments, and one day a hint you gave me at the opera, and which I have often thought on since—

CIDALISA.

You understood me, ungrateful man! and you did not answer it.

CLITANDER.

What could I do? Erastus, whose artifices you know, perceiving without doubt the impression you had made on me, and apprehensive that at last I might speak to you of it, came to me the next day with an air of profound mystery, and informed me that for above a month before you had engaged with him,

him, and that he had settled every thing with you, it was this false confidence which prevented me from understanding, and making you a suitable answer, and made me at last renew with Celimene.

CIDALISA.

Let us talk no more of him, I intreat you. you cannot conceive how much I am afflicted at the remembrance of it, nor how much I despise myself for my weakness in yielding to the most perfidious of men, to him whom, perhaps of all others, I was the least cut out for loving.

CLITANDER.

My own case exactly; who cannot imagine how I have taken up with Araminta, and a dozen other wretched creatures of the same sort.

CIDALISA.

Belisa, for instance.

CLITANDER.

She is at least pretty.

CIDA-

CIDALISA.

I agree with you; but then she is very common.

CLITANDER.

A little of that it must be confessed. Unhappily for herself, she has a sort of irresolution in her character, which exposes her to the inconvenience of not being able to give a denial, for bateing that, she would be pretty much like any other woman.

CIDALISA.

How came you to engage yourself with her?

CLITANDER.

I engage myself! I *had* her indeed, but without a moment's intention of keeping her. She was at the same time the woman in France whom I despised the most, and who cost me the least.

CIDALISA.

You *had* her, however.

CLITANDER.

Yes; but I could not help it. I went to pay her a visit, which I owed her for a long time: I knew not how she was disposed.

She

She made me advances, and those so lively, that, spite of all the contempt I entertained for her, at that moment, I could not help returning them. You cannot but know how horrible that is at bottom!

CIDALISA.

You think to laugh it off; but I assure you, there is nothing so infamous as to give way, as you all do, to every opportunity that offers.

CLITANDER.

You cannot imagine, likewise, how much we repent of those shameful weaknesses, when we find ourselves, as I confess was then my case, possessed with a violent and sincere passion for a woman, undoubtedly charming, since that woman was Aspasia.

CIDALISA.

I am very sure, in spite of all you say, that Belisa thought you was no body's but her's.

CLITANDER.

She is vain, I am amorous; and it is no wonder, in such circumstances, that we both deceived ourselves.

CIDALISA.

In the mean time you adored Aspasia.

CLITANDER.

Yes, and to madness!

CIDALISA.

But how could you reconcile your passion for her with those instances of complaisance you shewed to Belisa?

CLITANDER.

Oh! I had neither the insincerity to pretend to reconcile them, nor the misfortune to be deceived. Though loaded with favours from Belisa, and at a time too, when they made the liveliest impression on me, you cannot imagine how far she was from my heart, and how deeply I felt the sovereignty of Aspasia.

CIDALISA.

I believe it. You, however, saw Belisa again

CLITANDER.

Yes, she never had, as she said, supped at *petite maison*, and she asked it of me as a favour to give her an entertainment in mine.

mine. I could not, in the terms we then were, refuse humouring her in that whim. I will not even conceal from you, that she amused me for some time, and that all the reproaches I made myself on that head did not prevent me from keeping her a month. It is true, Aspasia was about half that time out of Paris, and it was at that time really necessary for me, that a woman I loved should not be so long absent.

CIDALISA.

Faithless creature!—Ah! let me alone then.

[*In order to understand this exclamation, which appears quite out of reason, it must be observed, that Citander is always plaguing Cidalisa one way or other fresh proposals, fresh refusals, complaints of Clitander, complaints of Cidalisa. She is, besides, obliged to complain of being too sensible, not to seem apprehensive that it may afford Clitander some reason for doubting his constancy. To assist the reader, what could be the meaning of what follows?*

CLITANDER.

It is a very odd notion indeed in you to imagine, I should find fault with you for your sensibility, when I had all the difficulty in the world to pardon the want of it in Celimene.

CIDALISA.

That is pleasant, to look at her, one would have thought her quite the reverse.

CLITANDER.

There are, however, few women colder than she is, and you cannot conceive how little in such cases physiognomy is to be depended on.

CIDALISA.

Have I the appearance of being sensible?

CLITANDER [*looking at her attentively.*]

Yes, you have a tender languor in your eyes which promises tolerably well.

CIDALISA.

Ah, you reduce me to despair! the thing in the world I dread the most, is to be thought so tender. You know not what you say. that languor you observe in my eyes

eyes may very well shew marks of a sensible heart; but it seems to me, it is only those women of an extraordinary vivacity whom you accuse of being—

CLITANDER.

Not your connoisseurs, and we leave it to young people just entering into the world to believe that all women have a great deal of that sensibility, and that it is chiefly found amongst those who have a great deal of fire in their eyes, great vivacity in their actions, and inconsiderateness in their conduct. As for us; languor, indolence, modesty, these are the charms that fix us.

CIDALISA.

You must then have been very urgent, very importunate with Celimene.

CLITANDER.

Much less so than you will imagine; whether it be whim or vanity, her greatest pleasure lies in raising desire she enjoys at least the transports of her lover, besides, the coldness of her senses prevents not her head from being all alive; and if nature has denied her what is called pleasure, she has given her in exchange a sort of voluptuousness which exists indeed only in her ideas; but which perhaps makes her feel something more delicate than what proceeds from the senses alone. As for you, still happier than her, you have, if I am not deceived, joined them both together.

CIDALISA.

I know not why; but I think I should rather choose Celimene's share than my own.

CLITANDER.

That is to say, you would be less happy by one half than you are be content. To whatsoever degree Celimene's ideas might be inflamed, and into whatsoever voluptuousness they might plunge her, she was not always satisfied. though she has the misfortune to be convinced that the bounds nature has imposed upon her cannot be broke through, she is yet extremely desirous of that intire enjoyment which nothing can procure her. Her imagination is in a combustion, she rebels against the coldness of her senses, and puts every thing in practice to overcome it, that ardour with which she burns,

and

and which spreads itself through her veins, becomes at last a punishment to her: and I have seen her oftener than once weep with vexation at being the victim of such violent desires, and unable either to extinguish or satisfy them.

CIDALISA.

If she could not, with you, arrive at the happiness she sought for, I would not advise her to seek it elsewhere.

CLITANDER.

I doubt, indeed, whether she has found it in her new choice, since it is a sort of an Erastus, who has banished me from her heart, therefore I am as little flattered as surprised at seeing her entertain some tender remembrances of me.

CIDALISA.

Will you take her again, Clitander?

CLITANDER.

As you will take Erastus again; with whom I doubt, that in some certain respects you are not intirely satisfied.

CIDA-

CIDALISA [*with an air of discontent.*]

It appears odd enough to me, that you should seem to believe that what you imagine him to be, should render him intolerable to me, when it was however himself that broke off our connection.

CLITANDER.

I am not surprised at that; these sort of lovers, who, besides, only pretend to it from affectation, after having teazed a woman intolerably, always conclude with leaving her, and even with as little ceremony, as if they had no occasion for her discretion.

CIDALISA.

After the manner you talk, you must have lived with very extraordinary women indeed!

CLITANDER.

Do not you believe that, I swear to you, except Aspasia and yourself, nothing can be so ordinary as those women who have honoured me with their favours.

CIDALISA.

But by what I see you have *had* several.

CLITANDER.

I have so, for what could I do? one is in the world, one is in a manner sick of it, one sees women, who, for their part, are not very busy one is young, and vanity and idleness go hand in hand. If to *have* a woman is not always pleasure, it is at least a sort of employment. Love, or what is called so, being unfortunately what pleases women the most, we do not find them always insensible to our assiduities. besides the transports of a lover are the surest proof they can produce of their worth. I have sometimes had nothing to do; I have met with women who perhaps were not yet very well assured of the power of their charms; and that has caused me, as you say, to *have* some of them.

CIDALISA.

What a pity! I think however, that you have told me oftener than once, as well as to night, that you never were a man very happy with the ladies.

CLITANDER.

I have not been so, at least, for a long time, and I can assure you, that I have at this day some difficulty to conceive how and

for

for what I could ever take up so painful and so despicable a trade. At first I could not help it, and through the whim of some woman, who then took the lead in the great world, I came to be all the fashion. The reputation my first adventures acquired me necessarily brought me into others; and without forming the project of *having* all women, it soon happened, that there were none in Paris, whom their vices rather than charms brought to the market, who did not think themselves obliged to *have* me, and I in my turn thought myself obliged to *have* them. In short, what would you have me say? my head was turned, and to such a degree, that had it not been Aspasia, whom at that time I addressed as I did all other women, but whose virtues I was forced to respect, and only became agreeable to her at last by endeavouring to imitate them, I should perhaps have been still involved in all those wild courses, which made me at that time so brilliant and so ridiculous.

CIDALISA.

You believe, then, you are perfectly reformed.

CLITANDER.

I believe it perhaps too readily; but in case Aspasia has left any thing to do, I am in your hands, and I know none so worthy to finish her work as the only person who, in her place, could have begun it.

CIDALISA [*kissing him.*]

Ah, Clitander! [*he torments her*] Have done then. I find I cannot thank you for any thing with impunity.

CLITANDER.

Am I then so very insupportable?

[*Fresh transports of Clitander. Cidalisa does not like them at first, but afterwards shares in them.*]

CIDALISA [*seeing him smile.*]

Ah, Clitander! when I am dying of love in your arms, does not my weakness afford you a very ridiculous spectacle?

CLITANDER.

I own I could never have thought you could have found any thing in my looks that could have brought on that reproach.

All that I know is, that if I found the same expression in yours, I should imagine I had much more reason to be thankful than complain of it.

CIDALISA.

Deceive me not, I conjure you, I shall not endeavour to make any panegyric on my heart, but, if you knew how sincere I am, and with what passion I love you, you would blush at loving me but moderately.

CLITANDER.

No, you do not love me, since you can make yourself uneasy about such trifles.

CIDALISA [*kissing him with transport.*]

I do not love you. Ah, my God!

CLITANDER [*pressing her in his arms*]

Be at ease then, I conjure you in my turn Consider, that your suspicions make me desperate. Let us enjoy the happiness of loving one another in tranquillity, and let that be the only business of our lives Yes, your sentiments alone can only equal mine; provided I can ever inspire you with the same passion you have done me.

CIDA-

CIDALISA.

Ah! do not suspect a heart intirely yours, and a woman who pardons her own errors, much less readily than yourself, and who is perhaps not even satisfied at seeing you so indifferent about the use she had made of her heart, before it was yours.

CLITANDER.

What! would you have me so unjust —

CIDALISA.

Yes, I would have you be unable to hear the names of Damis or Erastus mentioned without changing colour; that if I had the misfortune to meet them accidentally, you would reckon it no less a crime, than if I had made an assignation with them. If you but knew how odious those women you have loved, or only lived with, are to me, you would surely be angry at yourself for not looking upon these two men as your mortal enemies.

CLITANDER.

It would perhaps be still more unreasonable than dangerous to wish them so much ill for the sake of a happiness they no longer possess.

possess. I adore you! do not wish me to be jealous. If you knew to what excesses that passion carries one, you would not surely desire to find me so susceptible of it.

CIDALISA.

Ah! what does it signify? be unjust, suspicious, passionate; loaded continually with proofs of my affection; never think yourself sufficiently beloved. To whatever pitch you may carry your jealousy, you will never hear me complain of it.

[Clitander being still more the man of honour than Cidalisa would wish him to be, thinks it his duty to thank her for those proofs of her affection, but she makes so serious an opposition to this piece of politeness, that he is obliged to desist. He pouts at her; she kisses him, rallies him on his pretensions, and even ventures to assert, that it is not unlucky for his vanity, that she does not comply. This hint shocks him; he maintains, that vanity bears a smaller share than she imagines in the desire he has to return her thanks for the obliging things she has just said to him, and

as

as she continues obstinate in not believing him, he thinks himself obliged to give her convincing proofs, that she cannot reproach him with a lie. At last she does him justice, but so far from being better disposed to receive his acknowledgments as he desired, she assures him all she can do for him is to pity him He is a little out of humour at this pleasantry, and complains of her want of complaisance.

CLITANDER.

I did not imagine, I confess, you could have trifled in this manner on such a misfortune as mine. It is, let me tell you, a piece of barbarity without example.

CIDALISA.

That is but a poor jest. But, to comfort Araminta for the little value you set upon her charms, and your harsh treatment of her now, I have a strong fancy to tell her, as how you have proved yourself this night one of the most gallant cavaliers that ever received the gentle tribute of amorous gratitude. I believe she would be a good deal surprised at it.

CLITANDER.

No, she would not believe you, and indeed her vanity ought to render her very incredulous on that head.

CIDALISA.

Well, but tell me, had Julia as much reason to boast of you as Araminta?

CLITANDER.

So, there you are upon Julia again! it seems you still will have it, that I have *had* her. I do not believe however—

CIDALISA.

That you have *had* her, no doubt.

CLITANDER.

But though I should entertain some doubts on that head, they would be better founded than you may imagine; after all, I never had but one afternoon of her: and is that really what you can call having *had* a woman?

CIDALISA.

How! but an afternoon of such a woman! Julia! indeed, I should not have thought it.

CLITANDER.

Do not blame her, however; nothing would be so unjust. It would have been infamous in her to have kept me longer, and you yourself will be convinced of it, when you come to know how it happened. You remember the summer before last was excessively hot; on one of its sultriest days I paid her a visit, I found her alone in a room where all the blinds were shut, and the curtains being let down, darkened it still more; she was lying on a sopha in a very careless posture, and still more carelessly drest. A plain boddice but half laced, and a short under petticoat, were all she had on: her head was bare, and her hair, as well as the rest of her person, was in that sort of disorder which is a thousand times more alluring to us than any ornaments whatever, especially when, as in her, it is attended by the most scrupulous cleanliness, and all the graces of youth and beauty. You know how handsome she is; she had often tempted me, and by the bye, I had sometimes told her so. I never had so strong a desire, as to tell it her again that day. The attitude I surprised her in was charming; and I would

would advise every handsome woman to put herself in such another, when she wants to make the liveliest impression. Her petticoat, particularly, concealed but a small part of her limbs; no doubt, she was not ignorant of this: but, next to yours, they are the most perfect I ever saw; my coming in did not make her change her posture in the least. Just as I was going to tell her to what a degree I was struck with her charms, she began a conversation on the dreadful heat with which we had been suffocated for some days. You know that she has attended a course of physical lectures, and that she now-and-then gives a dinner to some members of the academy; and you will not wonder if, with all this, she thinks herself a perfect adept in natural philosophy. I had so often rallied her on the fancy she had taken for the sciences, that she thought she must not miss so fine an opportunity to convince me of her proficiency in them. She began then a long dissertation on the effects of heat, and that sort of lifelessness to which it reduces us, when it becomes extreme. That, as I remember, she pretended was occasioned by too great a dissipation of the spirits, and a relaxation of the fibres. I contradicted her,

she

she grew warm, and went so far at last as to maintain that there was not a man that very day, who would not find himself impotent in the arms of the finest woman in the world, though he loved her ever so passionately. At that very moment I myself could have given the most direct lie imaginable to her assertion; yet, whatever advantage I had over her, I contented myself with modestly saying, I was afraid she might be mistaken. My modesty and the gentleness of my voice persuaded her, in all appearance, that I had no good reason to be of a contrary opinion: this notion animating her with fresh courage, she told me confidently that she was sure of what she advanced, and that the first philosophers in the world were of the same opinion. I answered her still with the same gentleness, that it was not impossible for a man to be an excellent philosopher, and yet mistaken in this matter; that it might happen that those great men, whose authority she relied on, might have been determined only from their own experience; and that I, for my part, ventured to appeal from their judgment.

CIDA.

CIDALISA.

Surely! you could not have played philosophy a more villainous trick.

CLITANDER.

I ought to thank you for this, but perhaps you do not choose it.

CIDALISA.

That is to be considered, but go on with your story.

CLITANDER.

Very well; Julia growing still more confident in the opinion, and perhaps having had some secret experience in this article, which she did not venture to make use of as an argument to me, and which might yet be the real cause of her obstinacy, told me at last, with an air of vanity that shocked me, that if there were a man in the world on whom heat had not the effect which she alledged it must have, that that man must be a monster. You may imagine how much I, who had felt myself that monster for above a quarter of an hour, and who did not think myself a

very

very rare one, was astonished that she should prize a quality so much I made so little account of. Being very far from wishing to make an indecent use of it against her, I answered her still with the same humble tone, that I did not think any man, who had reasons within himself to be of a different opinion, ought to value himself much more for it. Upon this she said, but with an air that let me easily see how far she thought me from being furnished with such strong proofs against her system, that I was one of those ignorant fellows who take a pleasure in disputing against self-evident truths, and that often against their own internal conviction. My reply was, that miracles were not impossible; but I saw her so firmly determined to admit none of that sort, that I was at last obliged to convince her by ocular demonstration, that philosophers are not always in the right. She was struck dumb with surprise, and I never beheld a philosopher so deeply humbled. In the mean time, whether from pride or prejudice, reproaches succeeded soon to her confusion. Without being alarmed at them, I took the liberty to represent to her, that she had

had obliged me, by admitting none of my arguments, to have recourse to a demonstration, which might reduce her to silence, and to prove to her, that however general a rule might be, it always must be supposed to allow of some exceptions: I added, that for the honour of philosophy, and fully to convince her she had been mistaken, she could not dispense with pushing the experiment as far as it would go; that hitherto, I had only refuted one half of her system; and that it would be a disgrace to her to own herself overcome, when as yet there were only appearances against her, which might not be able to support a proof of a certain nature. The fear of being conquered too hastily, the wishes of humbling me in my turn, the oddness of the thing, the opportunity, the proof already offered, and which no contradiction could weaken, and more than all, no doubt, an earnest desire of instruction, got the better of those vain scruples that yet withheld her. A very tender sigh; that flushing in the face which desire and the expectation of pleasure produce, so different from that which proceeds from modesty alone, her eyes that sparkled with the liveliest passion,

and

and belied the severe air she had assumed; all, in short, informed me that she wanted nothing so much as to be instructed; and at the same time a sort of sneer, which I observed amidst all, let me also know that I should not easily get the better of her obstinacy. That I might not be interrupted in the important lessons I was going to give, I went to fasten the door, and returned impatient to demonstrate to her the falsehood of her opinions.

CIDALISA.

And you convinced her, no doubt.

CLITANDER.

Yes, but not without a good deal of trouble. However obstinate she had been, she gave out at last. It is true, I tormented her cruelly, but at the same time I undeceived her to some purpose.

CIDALISA.

Oh! I can trust you for that.

CLITANDER.

That is really very obliging, for instance—

CIDALISA.

I claim no merit from it, which perhaps you will not believe.

CLITANDER.

It is at least, what I could most earnestly wish not to be; suppose you should happen to be deceived?

CIDALISA.

That Julia should be deceived in deciding positively on what effect circumstances might have upon others, is common enough; but that I should be mistaken in my own feelings is impossible; however, be this as it will, you must finish your story. I have, I think, paid you so well for it, that you cannot in justice refuse to go through with it.

CLITANDER.

Though Julia be no great philosopher, that does not hinder her from being one of the most amiable women in the world, therefore I was extremely desirous that the course I had begun with her should not be confined to that day; and I pressed her very warmly to engage herself with me. Being

still

still more grateful for the pains I had taken to instruct her, than chagrined at my having detected her in an error, I should undoubtedly have succeeded, had not the violent passion she then bore for Cleon, and the fears that the learned intercourse I wanted to enter into with her, might be suspected by him, obliged her to refuse me. Persuaded, however, that after what had passed, I should easily find some favourable moment with her, I did not insist so far as to be troublesome, and we parted the best friends in the world. I have, however, ever since been seeking in vain for those opportunities, which I thought to have found with so little trouble. Without giving me any room to complain of her behaviour, she has only avoided being alone with me, as long as she perceived I had any attachment to her. Last winter, however, in spite of all her precautions, I met her by herself, at Lucilia's, the solitude we were in, renewed my desires, and the air of constraint she observed towards me, which I did not interpret properly, encouraged them. I asked her with a smile, whether she had any doubts on the manner that cold might affect us? She blushed; I fell at her knees, and said every pressing and tender thing that could be thought of; but she was more embarrassed than affected. The power she had given me over her, and which, by the liberties I ventured to take with her, she saw I but too well remembered, so far from seducing her senses, as I had flattered myself, served only to afflict her; not daring, after what had passed between us, to shew me a severity I might have thought ridiculous, and become desperate at the levity I treated her with, she fell a weeping bitterly. The thing in the world I have always detested the most, and what is, indeed, unworthy of a man of honour, is to triumph over a woman in such a manner as to humble her to herself. Sure of victory, and not doubting, that if I had used all the arguments she had furnished me with against herself, I should plunge her into the deepest affliction, I asked her pardon for what I had done, and desisted from what I had intended to do: she was so touched with a generosity my attempts had left her little room to expect, that, I believe, she would have granted me, out of gratitude, more than I had endeavoured to ravish from her, if, at the very moment, Lucilia had not come in. Good actions, however, go

seldom

seldom without their reward; and I was that very evening indemnified by Lucinda for the sacrifice I had made to Julia.

CIDALISA [*eagerly.*]

Ah, Clitander! if you love me, give me the story of Lucinda, of all women in the world I hate her the most, and I cannot express the joy I feel at the thoughts of something having happened to her, unbecoming that dignity of sentiment on which she values herself so much.

CLITANDER.

I am very willing to do you that pleasure, but I would not have you believe I shall give you one of my finest stories for nothing, especially when it has so greatly raised your curiosity.

CIDALISA [*tenderly.*]

You are a cruel man!

CLITANDER.

I grant, that in some measure, I take an unfair advantage of your keenness to hear that story, and that really it is not generous;

but I am determined you shall not have it cheaper than Julia's; and you are very happy I cannot set it at a higher price.

CIDALISA.

Very well; if to-morrow you will come and pass the night with me, we shall see.

CLITANDER.

If I will! what! can you doubt it? yes, I shall surely sleep with you to-morrow night, since you are willing to receive me into your arms; but you are sensible, what a cruel restraint must succeed to my transports; my eyes will not even dare express my feelings, or at least they ought not, how then can I answer that my desires, more irritated than satisfied, will not betray me? I feel it, and will not be answerable for myself, if I leave you in my present ecstasy of passion. Consider whom we have to deceive with respect to our mutual sentiments, people very malicious, and very knowing. Alas! how would you have me dissemble mine, when I cannot look upon you without the liveliest emotions; when your eyes cannot turn towards me without piercing me to the heart; when I cannot

cannot see you open your mouth without wishing to shut it with my lips; when every thing in short, on seeing you, will continually recall to my mind those pleasures you have blessed me with, and will throw me into an ungovernable impatience for fresh enjoyment? Suffer a more peaceable voluptuousness to preside in my heart, by leaving me more in tranquillity; you will not see me less amorous. whatever you can possibly grant to my passion, there will still remain but too much for my punishment.

CIDALISA.

Well, then be at peace,—enjoy all my tenderness, and those transports you inspire me with. You teach me, that, before you, I never was beloved; and I feel with more pleasure still, I never loved any one like yourself. You disturb—you pierce—you overwhelm my soul—but do you feel how much I love you?—I am no longer myself, I die with your passion and my own.

> [*Clitander's answer, however spirited it might have been, is here omitted. It is certain, all that lovers say between themselves is not fitted to be interesting*

interesting; and that sort of talk, which often amuses them the most, is the most difficult to be committed to writing, and the least worth the trouble. Their broken and interrupted discourses are therefore suppressed in this place, as well as in some others, and those only are set down which the reader, without giving himself much trouble, can understand something of.]

CIDALISA, [*on seeing Clitander still look at her with a threatning aspect.*]

Ah! are not you ashamed to be still so terrible? do not look upon me as you do, I beseech you; and if possible, leave me the peaceable enjoyment of our reciprocal sentiments.

CLITANDER.

What occasion of uneasiness do I give you now?

CIDALISA.

May not I find enough in the notion I see you entertain, that you shew me a great deal of love, and are wonderfully agreeable, when perhaps you only make me afraid.

CLITANDER.

You wrong me, by alledging I entertain these thoughts; I protest I have no such; I am intirely actuated by the impression your charms make on me, and do not in the least think the manner in which I express it, that, of all others, I might use, which ought to give you the most satisfaction: though, to tell the truth, if I did, I do not think it should be a reason with you for doubting my affection.

CIDALISA.

You have really a strange opinion of our sex; and I own I am not without apprehension of being one day the victim of it.

CLITANDER.

It is so far from being true, that I think of all women in the same manner, that I am not surprised at not receiving from you compliments on a merit, which, to the most respectable Araminta, appeared deserving of the highest applause.

CIDALISA.

I should be surprised, indeed, if we commended the same thing.

CLITANDER.

But I must likewise observe, without reckoning on the difference between her way of thinking and yours, that you do not lie under the same necessity.

CIDALISA.

I should be sorry, were it possible to make, without great injustice, the slightest comparison between us.

CLITANDER.

I do not believe, however liable you may be to terrors of another sort, I shall ever have occasion to cure you of that.

CIDALISA.

Indeed! but it is an odious woman, and I would fain believe, for the honour of my sex, that there are few like her.

CLITANDER.

There are of her sort, I believe, more than you think of, and fewer than we say.

CIDALISA.

But to come to the point; you owe me Lucinda's story.

CLITANDER.

No, upon second thoughts, it will not please you, I was only joking, when I said it would divert you; it is but a common simple affair, which I doubt will not be worth the trouble of telling. Imagine to yourself an adventure in a coach, one of those things that happen every day.

CIDALISA.

It is no matter, I must know it.

CLITANDER.

Confess then, that you seek rather to puzzle me, than divert yourself.

CIDALISA.

Be it so; but let me have it however.

CLITANDER.

That very same evening I met with Julia at Lucilia's, Orontes, I know not
for

for what, having quarrelled with Lucinda at supper, went away without giving her notice. As she depended on his carrying her home, and of course had not ordered her own carriage back, she was very justly piqued at his behaviour, and made me a proposal of setting her down. We had been acquainted for some time, and even at one interval she seemed to have had some views upon me. As soon as we were by ourselves, we both fell a railing against Orontes. She seemed so mortified at what had past, that I thought it my indispensable duty, being so sincerely her friend, both to advise her to take her revenge, and even to offer her my service for that purpose, besides, I endeavoured to make her consider that a resolution as the only one she could take in honour, after the cruel affront he had put upon her. I had no great difficulty in proving to her the necessity of taking a revenge, but to whatever pitch her anger was raised, I did not persuade her at first, so easily as I had flattered myself, that it behoved her to take it on the instant. In the mean time, I was pressed for time, I saw that if I gave her leisure to reflect, that I should

should lose her, or, supposing that she did not pardon Orontes for a fit of passion, which in all appearance proceeded only from jealousy, or something of less moment, that, to determine her in my favour, I must employ cares and assiduities I did not choose to be at the trouble of. I remembered, that one day, when talking of what is called *impertinence*, she blamed it only to a certain degree, and even added, by way of jest, that she thought it less offensive than indifference. But whatever hopes I might entertain, that an impertinence from me would hurt her less than from another, that method appeared somewhat violent, and impatient as I was, that she should determine, I thought it still my duty to remonstrate to her on the wrong she did herself by not taking her revenge. Whether desire made me more eloquent than common; whether, as it happens, but too often, to women in a fit of ill-humour, that reflection only heightened her anger, and for that reason she was more easily persuaded, I found her much better disposed to believe me, than she had been at first. As soon as I perceived her affected, I endeavoured to determine her in my favour, by addresses much more animated than I had hitherto made use of, and I pressed her not to hinder me making her reparation for the slightest affront, were it only the cause of anger she had against Orontes. As she gave me no answer, I thought it best to interpret her silence in my favour, and I acted in consequence. I shewed, indeed, little sentiment, but a great deal of ardour; and it is but too common, that the one stands in stead of the other, and often carries people much farther. She said at first, I was an impudent fellow; I knew it well, then, that she would cry out, but she did not, and though she had had recourse to so indecent a step, my coachman, unless I had cried out myself, would not have stopt. As I was obliged, however, to say something to Lucinda, I agreed with her, that, indeed, she might find me a little too free; but that love, desire (eternal excuses for all impertinencies that ever were, are, or will be committed) ought to justify me in her eyes; that besides, since one or the other had hurried me so far, that the more culpable I became, the more reasons I found to hug myself on account of my faults. I became

at

at last as faulty as possible. I know not whether it was the positive tone, that almost always imposes on you, or that at the same time that I found, as I told her, reasons for hugging myself for my faults, she likewise found reasons for my excuse; but she cooled so far as to tell me only, that it was ridiculous. Though I had not perceived by the softness of that expression, how much her anger against me was softened, I should not, for all that, have desisted from being faulty. In appearance she did not doubt it; but whatever were her thoughts on that head, one thing is certain, that before she got home, she was avenged.

CIDALISA.

But there is only one street from Lucilia's to her own house.

CLITANDER.

That's true, but it is a pretty long one; besides, my coachman knows the world so well, that whenever I have a woman with me by night, he always supposes I have some very interesting business with her, and therefore carries me a road as far about as he thinks I would order him, were I really to make him my confident. The way, by this management of his, became a good deal longer, and, though it had been really much shorter, such was her anger and my importunity, that she could not have helped being determined before she got to the end of it. In the mean time, whether she had reflected on the strange hurry of her revenge, or whether she was afraid that Orontes, naturally suspicious, might learn, that after carrying her home, I had gone in with her, we were no sooner at the gate, than she resumed her stately airs, and told me my behaviour was infamous, that while she lived, she never would trust herself again in a coach with me, and that she could not have thought me capable of such a piece of insolence to a woman of her rank. I readily owned, that I had been a little too hasty; that I could not myself conceive how I came to be so far wanting in respect to her, that I was dreadfully ashamed of it, and the more so, as such doings were as little familiar to me as to herself, and that I could assure her, she had been the first with whom I had forgot myself to that degree. I doubted whether such an excuse, however obligingly turned, might prove satisfactory: therefore I was not much

much surprised at her thanking me in a very spiteful peevish manner for the preference I had given her. Love! tender passionate love, was again my excuse, whilst she was scolding me, and among other severe things had said, that in all appearance I had taken her for an opera girl. My carriage entered the court, and I was preparing to lead her in with a great deal of respect, when she told me in a violent passion, she would not have me get down. I represented to her, at first very gently, that it would be very ridiculous in her to refuse me her hand, that her servants and mine would not know what to think of it; that she could not even shew any displeasure at me without the risk of letting them into the secret of what had happened; that she would ruin herself by such a piece of indiscretion, that I was too sincerely attached to her to suffer her to give way to passions that would be attended with such troublesome consequences; that besides, it was impossible for me to leave her before I had asked her a thousand pardons on my knees, and endeavoured, by my respectful penitence, to obtain her forgiveness. She made me no other answer, but by a furious attempt to throw herself out

out of the coach. I held her, and seeming in a paffion in my turn, told her, I would not fuffer her to ruin herfelf. Whether fhe pretended all this paffion in order to reinftate herfelf a little in my good opinion, or whether, which I cannot eafily believe, fhe was really ferious, it was a long time before I was able to appeafe her, at laft, when fhe was tired either of being angry, or only pretending to be fo, fhe told me, that fhe faw perfectly well into my project, that the defire of infulting her ftill farther had a greater fhare in my earneftnefs to wait on her, than any care I had for her reputation; but that fhe knew very well how to fcreen herfelf from my infolent attempts; and that fhe would not fpeak to me, but in the prefence of her women. Very well, madam, anfwered I with a determined tone, I fhall then have the pleafure of having them for witneffes of all thofe tranfports you infpire me with. Though this fhort anfwer, and the firmnefs of my tone, had a great effect upon her, fhe endeavoured, but in vain, to hide her apprehenfions from me, and anfwered me boldly, We fhall fee. So then, madam, replied I, pretending great vehemence, you will fee. upon

this

this we alighted from the carriage, I calling her my lady with the moſt familiar air in the world; and, that I might leave her in no doubt of my intention, graſping her hand with all my ſtrength. Oh! as much as you pleaſe, my lord, ſaid ſhe, in a whiſper, but you ſhall go for all that, I aſſure you: upon honour, returned I, I would not adviſe you to propoſe it, unleſs you want to expoſe yourſelf to a ſcene which may not prove very agreeable. As I have ſaid, I really frightened her, and her apprehenſions I might make a noiſe, determined her, but in all the ill humour imaginable, to carry me into the little apartment which you know, looks into the garden. At firſt ſhe fell a walking about in a ſort of fury. Certain ſhe would be ſoon tired of that, I made no oppoſition, but ſtood with my eyes caſt down, and in a ſolemn ſort of ſilence, waiting till ſhe ſhould ſit down. At laſt, ſhe threw herſelf on a great elbow chair, leaning her head on her hand, quite in the attitude of one who is in a profound *reverie*. As ſoon as I ſaw this, I threw myſelf at her feet: at firſt ſhe puſhed me back ſomewhat violently; at laſt, I ſeiſed the cruel hand that repulſed me, and devoured it with the

moſt

moſt eager kiſſes. She made ſome efforts to withdraw it, the ſoftneſs of which, amidſt all her endeavours, I eaſily perceived. I then ventured to claſp her in my arms, but rather with the affectionate tenderneſs of love, than the rough petulance of deſire. Though I never believed I ſhould have much difficulty with her, and that her anger had not much alarmed me, yet after the want of reſpect ſhe complained of, and which, to tell the truth, there was ſome foundation for, I could not but ſeem to believe her as much vexed as ſhe affected to be, without it may be putting her in a greater fury againſt me ſtill, than ſhe wanted to ſhew. I did not love her, but ſhe pleaſed me, and though ſhe had not made ſuch a reſiſtance to my impudent attempts, as to make me believe ſhe regarded them as a violence, yet ſhe had withheld all thoſe graces and delights that are inſeparable from conſent, in a word, I was not yet acquainted with her in ſome reſpects, and I was reſolved that nothing ſhould be wanting to my victory. Another, perhaps, would have endeavoured to excuſe his fault by throwing one half of it upon her, but though I knew perfectly well, that

it

it was her fault alone that I was not much less to blame, I generously put it all to the account of my impudence. While I was making her the profoundest protestations of respect, I removed, but with a seemingly trembling hand, a cloak which without telling a lie, hid from me some very pretty curiosities. I know not whether the genteel manner I went about it, which, indeed, testified a great deal of regard, prevented her from opposing my enterprises, or, whether being quite taken up with her anger, she did not think of what she was doing; but at last, this jealous cloak was no longer an obstruction to me. I had, surely, good reasons for passing compliments on what presented itself to my eyes, but I thought that transports would inform her better than compliments, of the impression they made on me, and accordingly I overwhelmed her with them. I believed, indeed, she would have some difficulty to reconcile the profound respect for her I boasted of to my passionate proceedings, and that she easily saw how much I was at variance with myself; but she thought in all appearance I was as sensible of it as herself, and that therefore it was needless to tell me

of

of it, or my tranfports, to which I joined from time to time all the gallantry imaginable, flattering her pride, and perhaps alarming her fenfes, fhe had not ftrength either to ftop them, or to make me take fhame to myfelf for my inconfiftence. Still appearing to make a refiftance, fhe began at laft to abandon herfelf into my arms. All my entreaties, however, had not yet been able to obtain a look; and, though I had no occafion to confult her eyes for a knowledge of her difpofitions, or an encouragement to take advantage of them, I was determined, as I told you, that nothing fhould be wanting to my triumph; and I tenderly preffed her to vouchfafe to honour with one glance an unfortunate man, who adored her. At laft I obtained that favour, and, as I had fufpected, found more trouble than anger in her eyes. This moment of goodnefs, on her part, paffed off like a flafh of lightning; I intreated therefore another favour of the fame fort; and my intreaties were not in vain. O! leave me, my lord, and if poffible, do not make me hate you more. However gently thefe words were pronounced, I could not

eafily

easily hear it said I was hated; and I took the liberty to ask her, if it was in that manner she pardoned? A smile, tenderer perhaps than she herself imagined, was all her answer, and you will not be at a loss to guess, how I thanked her lips for that smile. She so little expected a familiarity of that sort, that she had not time to contrive how I should obtain the appearance only of the favour I ravished from her, and which I enjoyed as deliciously as if she had granted it with all the good will in the world. This new happiness (for you may imagine, that in the chariot a thousand things had been forgotten) was not, however, without its alloy. If from time to time I had reason to congratulate myself on Lucinda's indulgence, she much oftener found means to make me sensible that I was doing her a violence; and though I easily perceived, that she was more in earnest in her desires than in her anger, yet the alternative hurt me, but how to tell her so, without giving her a liberty she might make a bad use of against me, was the question. In that case, I must have gone through a fresh round of reproaches on her side, and excuses on mine,

and

and thus spend, in such miserable doings, a time I could employ to much better purpose. I therefore thought, on reflection, the best way I could take to triumph over her perverseness was to be equally perverse in my turn, and I soon found it was not possible to doubt my being in the right. I no sooner found her as reasonable as I wished, than I laid aside those appearances of respect I had hitherto preserved in some respects, and I determined to see how far she would carry her clemency. At first, I did not find it as ample as I thought I might have flattered myself, and I had still some scruples to combat. Her resistance, in short, giving me more pain than pleasure, and being convinced, I had carried my complaisance farther than my situation required, I resolved with regret on the only stroke of authority, which could finally terminate this affair; and I met with all the expected success. It is true, Lucinda would have me still believe she was offended; but at last I saw her more in her real character than she wished to appear, forgetting at the same time that she loved Orontes, and did not love me, and experiencing in her revenge all those pleasures it is alledged she enjoys.

CIDA-

CIDALISA.

How is this, traitor! you told me this story would not divert me, and I think it charming.

CLITANDER.

Really, it is not absolutely bad. I fancy, however, that Lucinda herself would think it detestable: thus, you see one cannot please all the world; but give me one token at least, that you have some obligation to me for it.

CIDALISA.

No.

CLITANDER.

How? no!

CIDALISA.

Besides, it is not finished, this story, and I have not forgot that I payed you for it beforehand, and I want to see whether you owe me nothing for that.

CLITANDER.

But suppose I should not finish it.

CIDA-

CIDALISA.

I doubt whether I should be a great loser by it, and that you have not already told me all that is most interesting in it.

CLITANDER.

So then! but you are mistaken though; be that however as it will, nothing is more certain than that you shall not have the rest of it, but at the price you paid me for the beginning.

CIDALISA.

Do not talk to me in that manner; for seriously you terrify me. [*He wants to torment her.*] Oh, as for that, by no means, you shall catch me no more.

[*She takes all imaginable precautions against him.*]

CLITANDER.

So, this is excellent! there is fine doings indeed!

CIDALISA.

I am sorry you take it amiss; but, you may depend on it, for this night I shall behave no otherwise. Instead of tormenting
me

me as you do, and setting up the most ridiculous pretensions in the world, why don't you finish your story?

CLITANDER.

Well, since it must be so—but you fancy perhaps I am so complying, only because I find it more convenient for me than to carry it with a high hand against you. It is however no—

CIDALISA.

Oh, my God! I do you all the justice possible on that score.

CLITANDER.

It is because I would not have you believe—

CIDALISA.

O by no means; I believe nothing to your disadvantage; be quiet—Indeed, I dispense with your proofs. Very well, I am convinced; shall I have your story at last?

CLITANDER.

Whatever had been to blame in Lucinda and myself, being now so equally shared between us, that she could no longer, with any appearance of justice, call me impertinent,

she had no sooner recovered out of that absence of mind into which I had thrown her, than she cast down her eyes with marks of the greatest confusion. I was sensible, that at this time, the best way to soften those reproaches I saw she was going to load me with, was to put her in mind of Orontes's injurious treatment of her; I told her that one might pardon a private affront, but when a man forgot himself so far as to make it publick, it was then impossible to pass it over. I added, that I had never in my life-time seen a scene like that of this evening, and that she was the only woman who would have kept a lover so long, who had no other way of expressing his affection, but by such groundless jealousy and violent behaviour. This discourse had the effect upon her I expected: she took fire again, agreed that I was in the right, and flew out against him with all that vivacity which you know is natural to her, and was now only surprised that she had delayed so long in taking revenge of so troublesome and disrespectful a lover. In the same degree that she began to think herself less culpable, I became, as was reasonable, innocent in her eyes. The
eager

eager zeal I testified for her interest, I knew not what comparison she took in her head to draw between Orontes, and me, and, which at that moment turned to my advantage, a sort of taste which it may be she suddenly took for me, all forced her to assume that tender and familiar tone which I had hitherto wished for in vain. I answered her in that manner which might encourage it most; and though, to tell the truth, it was not on the part of sentiment that I shone most in this conversation, yet she discovered that I was the man of the age who possessed the greatest share of delicacy, and was besides surprised she had not found it out sooner. What had before appeared, with some shew of reason, a piece of the most enormous impudence, became very soon only a rashness, from which the most respectful lover cannot always keep himself free; one of those unhappy moments in which a man is hurried away in spite of himself, and which it is impossible for a woman not to forgive, when love, and not desire, is the motive. Although I was now sufficiently assured of my pardon, I was resolved she should grant me all that the impetuosity of my passion had hitherto

deprived me of, and that, in order to efface even the flightest impreffions of my impertinence, we fhould go through a regular progrefs of all thofe fteps our affair would have taken, had we had time to draw it out to a length from the beginning. I therefore told her, with all the paffion imaginable, that I adored her. Immediately a very tender confeffion rewarded me for what I had juft faid, attended with all thofe little favours that could confirm it; thefe again brought on others, and fhe now made no more refiftance than what ferved to increafe our pleafure. Love, indeed, entered but little in all this; but it was a long time before we were fenfible of its want. Though fhe has a thoufand charming things about her, infomuch that few women poffefs fo many, though fhe is lively, fenfible, and has numberlefs graces for a lover, every one more engaging than another, yet I know not how, by fome capricioufnefs of tafte, fhe feemed to me better fitted to amufe a man for fome time, than to fix him, perhaps neither of us perceived this. But how much foever morals and principle may be out of date at prefent, we ftill cannot help wifhing for
them.

them. I had, therefore, no inclination to keep her, unless (as when I do not love, nobody can have less pride) she had settled it in such a manner, that Orontes, or some one else, had saved me all the ceremonious part, and I had been suffered to remain in the crowd. Though I did not despair to bring her to an accommodation in this article, yet she said such tender things to me, and took so serious measures for futurity, that I knew not how to let her into a project which testified so little sentiment, and even esteem. It was indeed no difficult a matter with me to promise her still more than she required; but I did not choose to use her so ill, as make her break with a man, who was at least very necessary to her vanity; especially, when I did not care to supply his place. I was not, however, very solicitous to draw her out of an error, in which it was convenient for me she should remain at this time, and which, by excusing her own fondness, made her yield herself up to mine without fear, and even without a scruple. However lively the conversation had been betwixt us, I was assured it would not always keep up to that tone in which it had

begun,

begun, and I thought I had better wait for her moments of languor, before I unveiled my real intentions. As soon as that moment came, which, in spite of the pleasures I enjoyed, I waited for with impatience, I began a conversation on the despair Orontes would be reduced to, for losing entirely, by his own fault, the only woman who could render a man perfectly happy. She asked me, if I thought him so sensible; to which I answered in the affirmative, and that I doubted not he would die of grief. It must be then out of vanity, replied she, for from his behaviour, I cannot imagine he has any other motive. Oh! as to his being very much in love, returned I, it is impossible you can doubt it. Upon this I laid before her at great length, and in a very lively manner, all that Orontes had done, to prove that he had for her all the passion it was possible for a man to feel; and whilst I owned that he had been guilty of offences towards her, I made her observe, that there were none which could be imputed to indifference, that during the four years he had adored her, she had had nothing to reproach him with, but fits of jealousy, very

cruel

cruel and outrageous, indeed; but which were only singular in him on account of their violence and duration, seeing that every lover is faulty in that respect, more or less. The moment I mentioned Orontes, I saw her bend her brows, and such a change on her countenance, as if she gave me thereby to understand she did not want to hear me speak of a displeasing object; but when I began to dilate on the love he had for her, and on all he had done to testify how dear she was to him, insensibly and in spite of herself she took an interest in it, she fell into a profound *reverie*, and sighed heavily, and at last, when, whilst I was beseeching her to forget him, I drew a picture of his tenderness and other agreeable qualities, she could no longer refrain from tears, or be able to comprehend how she could have done him the injustice, as to doubt for a moment of her being adored by him.

CIDALISA.
In truth, you are strangely wicked!

CLITANDER.
What would you have me do? should I have kept her?

CIDALISA.

No, but you ought not to have *had* her.

CLITANDER.

That would have been better, undoubtedly; but not to mention that she is well enough for a man to have tried at having her, I wanted to be revenged of Orontes, who, during the time of my connection with Aspasia, had very indecently done every thing in his power to supplant me. I had swore not to miss the first opportunity that presented of testifying my acknowledgments to him; and I thought I could not do it better, than by restoring him his mistress, after what I had done.

CIDALISA.

Nothing, surely, was more judicious, nor more equitable.

CLITANDER.

Yes, indeed, I believe it was the only party I could take. My discourse, in the mean time, disconcerted Lucinda so much the more, that even while I was enlarging on the charms and tenderness of Orontes, I spoke

to her very paffionately of my own fentiments. I perceived, with a fecret pleafure, that fhe was not far from believing that fhe loved him to madnefs, and that fhe entertained a very reafonable hatred againſt me. I was no ſooner fenfible of this, than I thought myfelf intitled to refume thofe liberties with her, which, by our laſt arrangements, ought to be reckoned altogether things of courfe betwixt us; but which by the new revolution that had happened in her heart, it was impoffible for her to look upon otherwife than as criminal. With whatever addrefs fhe endeavoured to hide from me her concern, her remorfe, her new wifhes, and the reluctance with which fhe ſtill yielded to tranfports, which but a moment before were fo welcome to her, fhe infpired me with too little paffion, and I was too well acquainted with thefe things to be deceived by her. Neither my careffes, nor my proteſtations drew any other anfwer from her, than that falfe fmile, and that fort of complaifance which a woman fhews a lover who pleafes her no longer, and whom fhe dares not tell fo; filent, with eyes caſt down, refufing even when fhe feemed to grant,
wholly

wholly occupied with an object she had just before so intirely cast off; no, I never beheld humour and distaste shew themselves with so little management, and so much *naiveté*. A momentary instinct of pride made me regret that I had procured myself this pleasure, and I was on the point of rattling her most severely for that humiliation I had brought on myself. Happily for her, and myself, this impulse of folly was of no long duration; and far from being blinded with the manner in which she had raised my passions, or mistaking it for love, I knew how to make myself master of it, and to behave accordingly. Not being able to extricate myself from my present imbarasment, but by means of reproaches, I took care, that at least they should be decent and moderate, and that nothing too humiliating for her should have place in them. I had good reason to manage it so, for I was surely much more to blame than her, who would have suffered her resentment against Orontes to go no farther than complaints of him to me, or at most simple projects of revenge, if I had not taken advantage of the violent agitation I found her in, and

ravished

ravished favours from her, which it never would have entered into her head to grant me of her own accord. It was, therefore, without any gall or bitterness that I complained she had been mistaken with respect to the state of her heart, when she imagined I had made her forget Orontes. A look and a sigh, which informed me how deeply she reproached herself for having imagined so, were all my answer. I then said all the smooth and flattering things a man could say to a woman who had just quitted him ; and I told her, I was the less surprised at my present misfortune, because in the midst of the favours I had received from her, I still perceived how much she was attached to the man whom she seemed to sacrifice to me. I added, that it would yet be more mortifying, if that however were possible, for me to possess her against her inclination, than it would have been agreeable for me to have kept her with it : that, however much I might suffer, I should not imagine I had any right over her, from the moment she denied my title, and that I would rather preserve the barren name of her friend than

that

that of her lover, when it could only serve to make her life unhappy.

What strange creatures some women are! It is certain, after what had passed between us, and in her present situation, that nothing could be luckier for her, than the moderation with which I suffered her to cease loving me. I ought then naturally to have expected thanks for it: but she was more sensible of the injury I had seemed to do her beauty by this facility of disengaging myself from her, than of the sacrifice I had made her of my passion; and if she had the resolution not to complain of it, she could not, however, dissemble the mortification that her pride felt from it. I knew not, for some time, whether I should appear to take notice of this, or whether I should continue to pursue my first project, but the reflection, that all I could say on this head, would only serve to lengthen out this scene, and that whether she thought me amorous or indifferent, she would, nevertheless, return to her former taste, determined me for the latter party. After some tergiversations from her avenger, I became her confident: this second character did not flatter my vanity so much

much as the former, but, as it was more convenient for me, I beheld Lucinda, without any sort of chagrin, pass from the most furious love to the coldest indifference. What a revolution!

But, cruel love! these are thy tricks. Lucinda, in short, pushed her indifference so far, and conceived at the same time so great a confidence in my friendship, that she scrupled not to consult me on what measures she was to take. I answered with the same coolness, that from the moment I had consented to make a sacrifice of myself, nothing was so easy as her affair; that I flattered myself she would do me the justice not to doubt my discretion; but as it was possible that Orontes, who is really of a temper desperately jealous, might learn I had passed the night with her, and might torment himself on that score, if she seemed desirous of concealing it from him, I should go that very morning and call him to account for his capricious behaviour, and tell him, that I had in vain spent the greatest part of the night in persuading her to forgive him. She highly approved of my proposal, and promised me an eternal friendship.

CIDA-

CIDALISA.

That was surely very pretty on both sides, and this affair could not have ended more nobly.

CLITANDER.

Ended, say you? no, that it is not yet.

CIDALISA.

What, did she change her mind again! I thought it would be so.

CLITANDER.

No, by no means. What I have to tell you now is a greater beauty still, but, however admirable it may be, you shall not wait for it much longer.

Just as I was going to take my leave of Lucinda, after our mutual protestations of friendship had begun to grow very faint, a pleasant notion came into my head, to obtain favours from her once more, notwithstanding the ardent love she then felt for Orontes. As this thought appeared to me very singular, and very improbable to succeed, I was sensible I could not go about it with too much address: I pretended then to look

upon

upon her with greater emotion than ever; I sent forth heavy sighs, and cast my eyes up to heaven with such a look of sadness, as if I had been going to shed tears, then, as if transported out of myself by the violence of the passions that agitated me, I threw myself at her feet, and omitted nothing which might shew the despair I was reduced to by the sacrifice she had obliged me to make, and even scrupled not to add, it was more than probable, I should not be able to survive it. Had it been possible, that such doleful complaints had not affected her, yet her pride had been too much piqued at the ease with which I had detached myself from her, not to be infinitely sensible of my return. She prayed me then very seriously to continue to live. I conjured her, in my turn, if she really took an interest in my life, to receive me once more into her arms. This proposal seemed to surprise her, but, by her looks, I judged that she did not find it altogether absurd, and that she was not mortally offended at it. It is likewise possible that the necessity she lay under of managing me, and the fear I might revenge a refusal by some unseemly indiscretion, might have

some

some influence on the gentleness with which she received it. Be that however as it may, she answered me with all the goodness one could expect from a sincere friend, that my regret would only become the deeper by that means; and that if I were wise, I should rather think of extinguishing my passion, than seek to rekindle it. I agreed she was in the right, but I persisted nevertheless; and caprice, fear, or vanity, supplying the place of tenderness, and even of compassion; "At least, Clitander," said she preparing to oblige me, "remember that you will have it "so, and if my complaisance for you pro-"duces the effect I fear, benot so unjust as to "impute it to me." Thinking now that she had warned me sufficiently, she yielded with a pretty good grace. I must confess to you a trick that I played her, but I am afraid you will think it rather too much. it was at bottom only an experiment, and there is no law against things of that sort.

CIDALISA.

So far from it, they cannot but be useful; and besides it is the taste of the times.

CLITANDER.

You may easily judge, from what I have told you, that it was not only without love, but with very faint desires, that I importuned Lucinda to grant me this last proof of her friendship. It was therefore a thing of course, that I myself felt no very lively emotions, nor was her heart, any more than my own, in a more favourable disposition; and both of us began this affair without an attention so fixed, but what we might wander upon other objects. We remained both of us, for a pretty long time, in this sort of indifference, at last, I thought she began to view matters in a more interesting light. It was not that she loved me more than she had promised, but in all appearance she found herself better amused It came then into my head to see whether the mere machine carries it with so high a hand over the sentiment as many pretend; and to be well informed of that, at the very moment Lucinda seemed to have forgotten all nature, or to exist only for myself, "Ah, madam! "cried I, how happens it, that in such "transporting moments I cannot lose the

" remembrance of my rival, or cannot, at
" leaft, make you forget him, for, indeed,
" I fee but too well that the happy Orontes
" only can poffefs you. In defpair to fee
" yourfelf in my arms, you only figh after
" the happinefs of finding yourfelf again
" in his; and it will be in vain for me to
" flatter myfelf I can banifh him one mo-
" ment from your heart."

" Yes, Clitander, fhe anfwered boldly,
" you are in the right, I adore him."

And, what is more remarkable ftill, while fhe was making this tender declaration in favour of Orontes, fhe was fmothering me with the moft eager careffes, and giving me the ftrongeft proofs of fenfibility I could expect from any woman, even at that moment.

CIDALISA.

And you have concluded, from fo honourable a proof—

CLITANDER.

That women are not fo much in the wrong as we are apt to think, when they
tell

tell us, that the livelieſt pleaſures make not thoſe who poſſeſs a certain degree of delicacy forget the object with which their heart is engroſſed; and that, when that object does not procure them, it is nevertheleſs to him they would wiſh to be indebted for them. What a fine diſcovery is this! but to be convinced of it, it was neceſſary to make ſuch an experiment as I have been ſpeaking of.

CIDALISA.

Ah! you wicked man.

CLITANDER.

Why ſo? what can one do better than endeavour to cure one's ſelf of prejudices, eſpecially of thoſe in which others are ſo apt to be loſt? but to have done with Lucinda, I kept my word to her in every article; you are the only perſon to whom I have told this ſtory; I forced Orontes to confeſs himſelf in the fault, and made him fall at Lucinda's feet, and aſk her pardon for the injuſtice he had done her; I even interceded for him, and had the glory to ſee it put into the treaty concluded between them,

that

that it was on my account only that she made up matters with him. This adventure, in short, has afforded me a real pleasure, and I have never thought of it since without laughing at it.

CIDALISA.

And for me, I cannot hear you without trembling. You seem to profess with respect to women a libertinism and perfidy which give me the cruellest alarms, and make me repent sincerely of my weakness for you.

CLITANDER.

I shall tell you no more adventures, since the only use you make of them is to plague yourself, and in order to set bounds to your fears, I must set bounds to my confidence. I can, however, swear to you, and with the strictest truth, that I am naturally faithful, and that you will, I dare say, be astonished at my regularity.

CIDALISA.

Alas! God grant it. [*She rings her bell.*] Seven o'clock already!

CLITANDER.

As for myself, I seldom rise till ten, and I doubt whether I shall learn to be an earlier man with you. Besides, you must be sensible I cannot leave you till I have given you fresh assurances.

CIDALISA [*getting out of bed*]

And I protest I will call Grisette, sooner than suffer you to plague me any more.

CLITANDER.

O! no doubt, that would be fine! trust me, and come to bed again.

CIDALISA.

And my bed? you promised to make it for me.

CLITANDER.

With all my heart; I can say without vanity, that Grisette, famous as she is, does not make a bed better than me.

[*They make the bed.*]

CIDALISA.

Well, so much the better. I never had more occasion to lie easy.

CLITANDER.

That is to say, you will not be visible till somewhat of the latest.

CIDALISA.

O! very late, indeed. And I forbid you to tell any of the women here, especially Lucinda, that I am not stirring.

CLITANDER.

I do not see why you ought to be more afraid of her than any other. But this I am convinced of, that she has nothing to apprehend from me, and that since our adventure she has absolutely the same notion of me as Julia, though I have oftener than once attempted to make her live with me in that free manner, which would have both suited the desires she inspired me with, and the small share of love I felt for her.

CIDALISA.

It is, indeed, singular enough, she should not lend ear to so reasonable a proposal.

CLITANDER.

It is so, and perhaps, more extraordinary than you think of. Very well, what say you of your bed?

CIDALISA.

That I never saw it better made. I am really surprised to see you possessed of this good quality.

CLITANDER.

Perhaps it appears superfluous to you; but I assure you, that till a certain age, there are few qualifications more necessary than this.

CIDALISA.

You do well to boast of it. I assure you, I do not esteem you a bit the more on that account.

CLITANDER.

I see you are not disposed to make me any acknowledgments; and I think, to punish you for your ingratitude, I may be allowed to spoil a work for which you give me so little credit.

CIDALISA.

O! that would be dreadful! when, had it not been for you, I should have been much better accommodated, without owing you the smallest obligation.

CLITANDER.

You have insulted me.

CIDALISA.

Very well, I shall push the affront as far as it will go. I fear you not.

CLITANDER.

I find in this challenge more courage than prudence, if I may be permitted to say so, but is it only to have the pleasure of being conquered, that you give me this defiance?

CIDALISA.

Not absolutely so; but is it really true, that my confidence is so ill grounded?

CLITANDER.

I flattered myself, that I had corrected you of all such doubts by examples.

CIDALISA.

Indeed, if I must speak seriously, I have none.

CLITANDER.

Is not this, however, somewhat ambiguous? will, you do me justice? Have you not done me an injury? ah! this doubt torments me too much for me not to rid you of it.

[*He takes his revenge.*]

CIDALISA.

Ah, Clitander! I ask you pardon.

CLITANDER.

It is good time.

CIDALISA.

Indeed, you are really too vain.——— A bed that was the best made of any in the world.———You are, I protest, insupportable!

CLITANDER.

Do you find————

[The reader ought not to conclude, from what Cidalisa says, that she chides Clitander seriously. It is true, she may be a little out of humour. (Ah! who would not have been so in her situation?) but it is, at least, equally true, that she is in the end thoroughly reconciled to him.]

CIDALISA.

Will you go, then?

CLITANDER.

If you will have it so, I certainly must; but I cannot help telling you, that in such cases, I have not been used to be sent away so early.

CIDALISA.

That may be; but I beseech you go now.
[He opens the door.]
O! Clitander, softly, I pray you.

CLITANDER.

Another good quality I have is to open a door the softest that can be imagined, and that I walk with a lightness that is incredible.

CIDALISA.

Alas! you possess but too many good qualities; and if it depended on me, I would willingly give all those you make such account of, for the certainty of your being constant and faithful to me.

CLITANDER.

Oh! no doubt you would make a good bargain. Go, my angel, I will assure you of that at a less expence. [*He tenderly kisses her hand.*] Farewell, may you, if possible, love me as much as you are beloved.

FINIS.

CPSIA information can be obtained at www.ICGtesting.com
Printed in the USA
BVOW01s1052180814

363275BV00021B/873/P